P9-BZQ-223

BOUNDARIES

How the
MASON-DIXON LINE
settled a
FAMILY FEUD

divided a
NATION

Sally M. Walker

CANDLEWICK PRESS

FOR HILARY,
whose idea started this adventure

First edition 2014

Library of Congress Catalog Card Number 2013946612
ISBN 978-0-7636-5612-6

13 14 15 16 17 18 TLF 10 9 8 7 6 5 4 3 2 1

Printed in Dongguan, Guangdong, China

This book was typeset in Baskerville MT.

Candlewick Press
99 Dover Street
Somerville, Massachusetts 02144

visit us at www.candlewick.com

CONTENTS

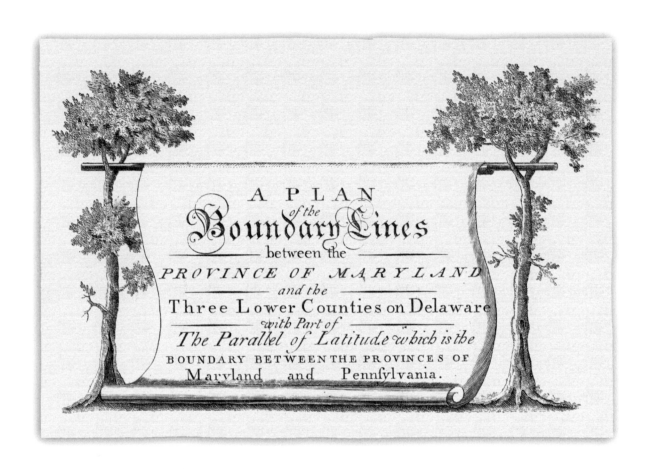

INTRODUCTION

W E LIVE IN A WORLD OF BOUNDARIES.
Boundary stories are plentiful in newspapers, on television, and on the Internet. A country at war with itself divides into two separate nations. Religious boundaries lead to persecution. Cultural boundaries reflect the rich texture of diversity but also the tensions that arise when people misunderstand or misinterpret societal differences. Scientific boundaries range from the ethics of cloning to the exploration of new galaxies. All these boundaries — how they change and how they don't — shape our world and who we are, as individuals and as members of the world community.

The story of the Mason-Dixon Line encompasses many different boundaries, some hundreds of years old. It begins with a country and the religious persecution of its own people. It becomes a property dispute. An escalating clash across cultural boundaries is part of the tale. So is surpassing a scientific boundary to achieve a feat many people deemed impossible. The line's story slices through history and helps us understand how human perceptions and the course of a country change over time. It's the story of how a political boundary became a symbol of freedom that helped shape the history of the United States. The tale of the Mason-Dixon Line reminds us to question the boundaries that surround us. And because it does, it is a tale for all times.

In some ways, the tale of the Mason-Dixon Line is a story of twos: two feuding families, two colonies in America, two kings named Charles, and two adventuresome surveyors. It's also the tale of how nighttime skies steered daytime courses. To fully know the Mason-Dixon Line's boundaries, you must know its roots. They begin in faraway places, then twist and turn in surprising new directions. They wind through heartbreak and triumph. And sometimes, without warning, they unexpectedly veer into danger.

Chapter One

OLD-WORLD PREJUDICE, NEW-WORLD DREAMS

MEET THE CALVERTS

The Calvert family was very familiar with boundaries and their restrictions. Even before his birth, in 1579, religious boundaries controlled George Calvert's life. His parents, Leonard and Alicia, were Roman Catholics. For them, worshipping publicly in England was illegal. As a little boy, George Calvert saw the Protestant authorities of Yorkshire force his father to conform to the Anglican Church. Had he refused, government jobs would have been closed to him and English society would have ostracized his family. He could even have faced imprisonment. Four years after his mother's death, George Calvert watched the same authorities similarly pressure his stepmother, who *did* refuse to conform. In reprisal, the authorities ordered Leonard to send twelve-year-old George and his younger brother, Christopher, to a village miles away from home, where a Protestant tutor would educate them.

George Calvert, the first Lord Baltimore, would come to have ambitious plans for a colony in America.

When he was a teenager, George Calvert was, as his father had been, ordered to conform to the Anglican Church. The pressure was intense. If George failed to cross this religious boundary, certain futures would become impossible. He could never attend university—that was forbidden to Catholics. Nor could he hold a government job. Yet English society expected a boy with the Calvert family's status to do both. George understood that, like his father, he had little choice. He complied and attended Anglican services. He never spoke publicly about how this made him feel.

CATHOLICS AND PROTESTANTS

*I*N THE EARLY PART *of the sixteenth century, the Roman Catholic Church festered with dissension about religious beliefs and practices. A group called Protestants split from the Roman Catholic Church and established Protestant denominations. For political and personal reasons, England's King Henry VIII renounced the Catholic Church and in 1534 established the Protestant Anglican Church—also called the Church of England—as the country's official church. Religious and political matters were not separated. English Protestants believed a person could be a loyal British subject only if he or she was a member of the Anglican Church. According to them, Catholics, such as the Calverts, placed loyalty to their religious leader, the pope, above loyalty to England. As a result, most Protestants regarded Catholics with mistrust and suspicion. Just ten years before George Calvert was born, one Englishman described the Calverts' predominantly Catholic neighborhood in Yorkshire as "evil in religion."*

Politics, death, and hope

George Calvert graduated from Oxford University, studied law in London, and began his political career in 1603 as the private secretary to Sir Robert Cecil, secretary of state to King James I. The following year, George married Anne Mynne, and a year later, their son Cecil was born. He and the many siblings who followed were all baptized into the Anglican Church.

As a discreet, skilled diplomat, Calvert quickly earned King James's respect. He was knighted in 1617 and two years later was named one of England's two secretaries of state. He bought a country estate in Yorkshire and planned the construction of his home there, Kiplin Hall. In 1621, Calvert thought beyond English boundaries and bought land in the New World, in Newfoundland, today a province of Canada. He expected that business ventures importing fish, timber, and other natural resources from Newfoundland would further enrich him and raise the Calvert family's status.

Kiplin Hall, George Calvert's country house, reflected his increasing power and wealth.

George Calvert and other Englishmen weren't alone in purchasing land in the New World. French explorers had navigated the Saint Lawrence River. Spain and Portugal had established settlements in the Caribbean and Mexico in the fifteenth century. During the sixteenth and seventeenth centuries, Spanish and Portuguese slave traders took African captives to the New World. In August 1619—the same year George Calvert became a secretary of state—the first Africans arrived in the Virginia colony, in America, when two planters traded food supplies for the "20. and odd Negroes" on board Captain Jope's ship the *White Lion*. But in 1620, when George Calvert purchased his Newfoundland property, people living in Virginia were not on his mind.

Juggling business ventures, construction, and politics consumed all Calvert's time. In London, he was King James's advocate for a political alliance called the Spanish Match. The king sought a political advantage by having his son, Prince Charles, marry the youngest daughter of Spain's king Philip III. But King Philip and his family were Catholics. Fearing that this connection to Catholicism might threaten Anglican boundaries and influence British policies, the Spanish Match was highly unpopular with Parliament, England's governing body.

In August 1622, tragedy struck the Calvert family: Anne died in childbirth. Losing Anne, who was "the dear companion and only comfort" of his life, devastated George. Yet his ten children needed love and care; he had no choice but to carry on.

The following year, when King James granted him a royal charter for a large tract of land in Newfoundland, Calvert's ambitions grew. A royal charter gives certain rights and privileges to a person or a company. The charter granted Calvert the right to establish his own colony, the Province of Avalon. As Avalon's lord proprietor, Calvert swore allegiance to the king but had the power to rule his colony independently—to set his own boundaries. Even as Calvert received the Avalon charter, he lost favor

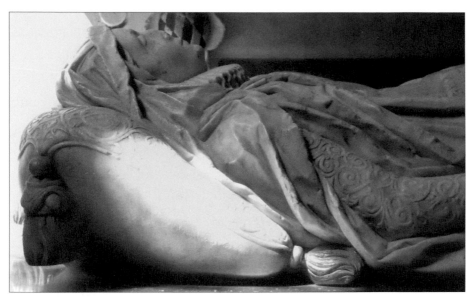

The alabaster sculpture on the tomb of Anne Mynne Calvert, the first Lady Baltimore, is a richly detailed likeness of her. She died giving birth to her eleventh child, who also died.

with Parliament over the Spanish Match and his friendship with Spanish Catholics. In February 1625, he resigned his position as secretary of state.

And then, making no public explanation, George Calvert converted back to Catholicism. His decision shocked his former colleagues. Yet King James did not withdraw his personal support. He publicly acknowledged his continuing regard for Calvert by granting him a manor in Ireland and the title Lord Baltimore. After King James's death, in March 1625, his son, King Charles I, acceded to parliamentary pressure and approved increasingly anti-Catholic policies. This may be why Calvert soon moved his family to Ireland, which was predominantly Catholic.

Good reports from his agents in Newfoundland convinced Calvert that his family's future was in the New World. In Avalon, he would make money, enriching his family, the king, and England. But Calvert sought more than riches and power. He wanted to change the boundary between politics and religion. He intended to prove to Protestant doubters that a Roman Catholic could also be a loyal British subject.

AVALON

In June 1627, when the Calverts visited Avalon, they found the colony deserted. George's agents had lied about the colony's progress and left. Still, Calvert remained hopeful that the colony would be successful, particularly if he assumed on-site control. He also pushed England's religious boundary with a daring move: he let the Catholic priests who accompanied him to Avalon hold Mass in one end of his house while allowing Protestants to hold services in the other. This never would have been permitted in England. In Avalon, however, Calvert had the authority to do so.

Calvert moved his family to Avalon permanently in 1628. Twenty-three-year-old Cecil, George's oldest son and heir, remained in England with his bride, Anne Arundell. While the rest of the family struggled in Avalon, Cecil managed the family's English properties and, in his own right, gained the respect of King Charles I and other members of government.

Despite George's hard work and high hopes, Avalon did not live up to his dreams. In a letter to King Charles, he wrote despairingly of the winter of 1628 to 1629: "from the middst of October to the middst of May there is a sadd face of wynter upon all this land. . . . My house hath beene an hospital all this wynter . . . of 100 persons, 50 [are] sick at a tyme, my self being one and nyne or ten of them dyed."

Unwavering in his dream of a New World colony, Calvert ended his letter, "I am determined . . . to remove my self with some 40 persons to your Majesty's dominion of Virginia, where if your Majesty will please to grant me a precinct of land with such privileges as the King your father my gracious master was pleased to grant me here [in Newfoundland], I shall endevor to the utmost of my power to deserve it."

Moving south

In the seventeenth century, smoking was the new rage in England. By the time the Calverts arrived in Virginia, in September 1629, English planters in the Virginia colony were already growing tobacco—a New World plant as profitable as gold.

George Calvert liked what he saw as he sailed toward Chesapeake Bay. By October 1629, he was on his way to England to persuade King Charles I to grant him a second royal charter, this time for a colony on Chesapeake Bay. In establishing this colony, though, Calvert had even more ambitious boundaries in mind. In his new colony, religion and politics would be separate.

For three years, George Calvert, his son Cecil, and influential government friends meticulously crafted and negotiated the terms of Calvert's colonial charter with King Charles I. Recognizing the benefits—goods from Calvert's colony would fatten not only England's purse but also his own—King Charles I approved. He declared George Calvert, Lord Baltimore, the colony's lord proprietor. This meant that when George died, his heirs would inherit the title and the colony. By the spring of 1632, the charter for the Province of

Cecil Calvert and his grandson Cecil, who visited England in 1669–1670. The other boy, whose name is unknown, was likely a family servant.

Maryland—named in honor of King Charles's wife, Queen Henrietta Maria—needed only final approval and official seals. There was one major difference between the charters for Avalon and Maryland: the stated intent to bring Christianity to the Indians living there. Ironically, even as Calvert removed a religious boundary and granted religious freedom to his colonists, he was required to convert the local native people to the Christian faith.

And then, with his colonial dream on the verge of reality, George Calvert fell seriously ill. He died on April 15, 1632, before the charter was passed. Achieving George's dream of a Maryland colony was left to his son Cecil, who became the second Lord Baltimore upon his father's death.

Chapter Two

MARYLAND'S SHORES

ON JUNE 20, 1632, when the charter for Maryland was signed and sealed, Cecil Calvert, although he lived in England, became lord proprietor of the Province of Maryland. Although Cecil had the right to set political and religious boundaries for Maryland, King Charles had the right to set its geographical boundaries. The charter partially describes Maryland as a peninsula surrounded by the Atlantic Ocean on the east, Chesapeake Bay on the west, and the Potomac River to the south. The colony's northern boundary was described as that land "which lieth under the Fortieth Degree of Northern Latitude . . . where New England ends."

At that time, King Charles I, the Calverts, and even English mapmakers had no specific knowledge of exactly which lands the fortieth degree of latitude crossed. Consequently, none of them had any idea of the huge fuss forty degrees north latitude would cause in the future.

George Alsop, an indentured servant in Maryland from 1648 to 1652, drew this map in 1666. It gave Europeans a tantalizing glimpse of the colonial frontier along Chesapeake Bay.

A DARING DESIGN

As lord proprietor, Cecil established Maryland on three foundations that he and his father believed to be crucial. The first—that colonists could acquire their own land—served a twofold purpose: it extended the English empire, and it gave the colonists property so they could increase their wealth. Loyalty to England and to the lord proprietor was the colony's second foundation. The third foundation concerned religious boundaries.

Unlike England, Maryland would have no official established religion. To assure that religion would be a private matter, Cecil instituted a daring policy called liberty of conscience. Under this policy, as long as a colonist was loyal to the lord proprietor, no government positions would be withheld from him because of his religious beliefs. Nor would a colonist be granted any special privileges because of his or her religious beliefs. Liberty of conscience was an unheard-of freedom in seventeenth-century England. Yet as soon as Cecil's colonists reached Maryland's shores, they would have it.

HIGH SEAS AND NEW NEIGHBORS

In November 1633, two ships, the *Ark* and the *Dove*, containing about 140 colonists—a mixture of Catholics and Protestants—left England for Maryland. Cecil Calvert and his family, however, remained in England, where Cecil felt he could best defend Maryland's charter from political rivals. Leonard Calvert, Cecil's twenty-seven-year-old brother, was one of the colonists; Cecil had appointed him as the province's first governor. Also on board were priests who belonged to the Catholic religious order known as the Society of Jesus, or, more simply, as the Jesuits. Led by Father Andrew White, the Jesuits were there to fulfill the charter's mission of converting native inhabitants to Christianity. To avoid conflict with the Protestants, the priests paid their own way and were subject to the same conditions as the other free colonists on the voyage.

Cecil Calvert recognized the likelihood of religious tension between Catholic and Protestant colonists and sought to forestall it in a letter of instructions. In it, he directed Leonard and other officials "to preserve unity and peace amongst all the passengers on Shipp-board, and that they suffer no scandall nor offence to be given to any of the Protestants, whereby any just complaint may heereafter be made, by them, in Virginia or in England." He requested that all observance of the Catholic religion "be done as privately as may be." Furthermore, Catholic colonists were not to discuss or debate religion, and government officials were to "treate the Protestants with as much mildness and favor as Justice will permitt."

The *Maryland Dove* is a replica of a seventeenth-century merchant ship. She is named after the *Dove*, which carried supplies to Maryland in 1634.

In early March 1634, three months after leaving England, the *Ark* and the *Dove* sailed into Chesapeake Bay, described by Father White as "the most delightfull water I ever saw."

While the waters of the bay delighted the colonists, the first view of their new neighbors may have worried them. Father White noted, "At our first comeing we found . . . the king of Pascatoway had drawne together 500 bowmen, great fires were made by night over all the Country." As Native Americans observed the *Ark* and the *Dove,* they felt a similar unease. News that the English "came in a Canow as bigg as an Iland, with so many men, as trees were in a wood, with great terrour unto them all" quickly spread among native villages. Neither group knew what to expect.

The *Ark* and the *Dove* sailed up the Potomac River and landed at Saint Clements Island, where officials erected a cross and claimed the land. Later, accompanied by an interpreter, Leonard Calvert journeyed farther inland and met with the leader of the Pascatoways, who according to Father White "gave leave to us to sett downe where we pleased."

The colonists chose a settlement site along the Saint Mary's River, near the mouth of the Potomac. They traded "axes, hoes, cloth and hatchets" with the Yaocomico Indians in exchange for a large parcel of land along the river's shore. For several months, the Yaocomico people and the English colonists shared the site, which the English named Saint Mary's City. This site and the Virginia colony's Jamestown were the only two English towns in the Chesapeake Bay area.

Yaocomico homes and storehouses were constructed of frames of bent saplings, which were then covered with mats made of wetland reeds called phragmites.

Moving forward

Slowly, Maryland gained a toehold in America. Managing the colony long-distance, Cecil assigned manor lands to a select group of his colonists, who either paid for the land outright or rented it. They tendered part of every crop to the lord proprietor. In ten years, the colony's population grew to between five and six hundred settlers.

Life in Maryland wasn't easy. Building and sustaining a colonial homestead meant that everyone, even the wealthy, worked. Additionally, tobacco is a labor-intensive crop. All planters who could afford to hired help, mostly males. From 1634 to 1635, men outnumbered women six to one. During the second half of the seventeenth century, as other types of labor increased and as families were established, the ratio dropped to three to one.

A SERVANT WORKFORCE

ALTHOUGH SOME FAMILIES immigrated to the new colony of Maryland, most colonists were individuals seeking prosperous lives. Most of the early immigrants could not read or write. But public documents such as court records, wills, and estate inventories provide records of their lives. During the first half of the seventeenth century, the majority of Maryland's workforce came from England as indentured servants enticed to the colony with the promise of fifty acres of land at the end of their indenture. These people signed a legal document called an indenture, in which they agreed to work for a landowner (called the master) for a specific length of time, usually four to five years. In return, the master paid the servant's passage to Maryland and fed and housed him or her during the period of indenture. A master could sell an indenture to a third party if he or she so desired. The majority of indentured servants were seventeen to twenty-eight years old.

While most of the servants were English, some were African. During the first half of the seventeenth century, the English did not commonly use the term slave. All African and European workers, regardless of legal status, were called servants. In seventeenth-century English America, slavery was not hereditary, nor was it always a lifetime condition. A predetermined time limit could be set, although the term was often so long as to make freedom unlikely. Most of the Africans were slaves, but some were freemen. Others served as indentured servants for the term of their indenture and were then free of further obligation to the landowner.

As much as Cecil Calvert wished he could go to Maryland, he felt that he could best protect his colony's boundaries, both geographical and religious, by remaining in England, where he lobbied endlessly on Maryland's behalf. Leonard's regular reports kept Cecil abreast of operations in the colony. While tobacco was Maryland's chief cash crop, Cecil requested that Leonard also send goods such as timber and animal hides. Sometimes, though, his requests went unfulfilled. In April 1638, Leonard regretfully wrote, "The cedar you writt for . . . I could not procure to send this yeare by reason there is very few to be fownd that are usefull tymber trees." Ships loaded with trade goods regularly sailed between America and England.

While wild animals—such as wolves, bears, and mountain lions—roamed Maryland's forests, domesticated animals, specifically hogs and cattle, also posed a threat to a colonist's survival, as they could wreak havoc on crucial food crops. The solution? Fences—although, in contrast to modern fencing practices, Marylanders enclosed their gardens rather than their livestock. Loose pigs and cows fended for themselves in the countryside. Colonists notched the animals' ears in different patterns to indicate individual ownership.

Colonists protected their crops by weaving branches to form wattle fences that were pig-tight, horse-high, and bull-strong. The fence in the background is constructed with split rails.

This replica of a seventeenth-century Maryland tenant farmer's home is located in Saint Mary's City. Its walls and roof are covered in clapboard, and it has a loft for storage and sleeping. The chimney is made of wattle and daub.

Acre by acre, Marylanders carved their place in America. And perhaps most important to Cecil Calvert, Catholics worshiped openly in Saint Mary's City, fulfilling the dream of liberty of conscience that his father and he had shared. However, religious tensions between Protestant and Catholic Marylanders grew. Some Protestants worried that the Jesuit priests who were preaching in Indian villages might turn the native inhabitants against the Protestants. Maryland's Protestants and Catholics argued about ongoing disagreements in England between the king and Parliament. Colonists grumbled about some of Lord Baltimore's policies concerning land grants in the province. Gradually, these tensions began to threaten the very survival of the province's unique policy.

THE SEASONING TIME

DEATH WAS NO STRANGER to Maryland's colonists. Swampy conditions and impure water caused fevers and diseases, such as dysentery, that killed many immigrants within weeks of their arrival. Changes in climate and diet, plus a harsh work routine, led to more deaths. Those who survived this period, which the colonists called the "seasoning time," could expect a hard life. Seventy percent of the men died before age fifty. Women had an even shorter life span. Twenty-five percent of the babies died during their first year, and half of those who survived infancy died before they reached the age of twenty. Most children lost at least one parent. Step and half brothers and sisters became very common due to the remarriage of the surviving parent. And the court assigned orphans without relatives to new families, for whom they worked in return for room and board.

A COUNTRY AT WAR

Troubled times in Maryland reflected troubled times in England. In London, conflict reigned between King Charles I and Parliament. Believing his right to rule came directly from God, King Charles claimed that he alone was best qualified to make important governmental decisions. Many members of Parliament, including a group of Protestants called Puritans, disagreed with this assertion and with some of the king's religious and political policies. The Puritans also disapproved of plays, music, and dance, all pastimes loved by Queen Henrietta Maria (a Catholic) and the king.

As Parliament sought reform in politics and in the Anglican Church, the gulf between it and the king widened. Three times, King Charles I angrily dissolved Parliament and ruled England himself. When he finally reinstated Parliament, in 1640, general battle lines for a civil war were already drawn: Puritans, merchants, and the Royal Navy supported Parliament; the aristocracy, the Anglican Church, peasants, and Catholics supported the king.

Fearing for their safety, Charles and the royal family left London in January 1642 under the protection of Royalist troops. Oliver Cromwell, a Puritan and a very powerful member of Parliament, remained in London, where he served as a commander of parliamentary forces.

In 1644, as England's civil war intensified, Cecil Calvert, perpetually strapped for cash, busily juggled the governing of Maryland even as he safeguarded his family's safety and position in England. That same year, William Penn was born in London. Less than forty years later, he would seriously threaten the Calvert family's boundaries in America.

Chapter Three

CONVICTIONS AND CONSCIENCE

IN SOME WAYS, William Penn understood boundaries even better than George Calvert had. By the time he was twenty-five years old, Penn had fought parental boundaries, defended the beliefs of his religion's boundaries, and challenged the legal boundaries of the British court.

Prior to Penn's birth, England's civil war placed his father, William senior, in a quandary. The Penn family had long supported England's joint rule by king and Parliament. So on the one hand, William senior was loyal to King Charles I and hoped that he and Parliament would reconcile. On the other hand, William was a captain in the Royal Navy, which was supported by Parliament. Professional commitments edged out personal beliefs. In order to keep his command (and stay out of prison), William senior had to fight the king's men. Eventually, parliamentary forces defeated King Charles's troops, and King Charles I was imprisoned in 1647.

While his father fought at sea, William Penn's mother, Margaret, anchored the family in their house on Tower Hill. From their house, she could see the infamous Tower of London, where many political prisoners had been jailed and executed. She nursed three-year-old William through smallpox. William survived, but as a consequence of the disease, he lost most of his hair. Margaret soon had him fitted with a wig. Although William's hair did eventually grow back, it did so sparsely. William wore various styles of wigs for the rest of his life. This was not problematic, since wigs were the fashion for men at that time anyway.

A DREADED DISEASE

JUST HEARING the word smallpox *struck terror in the hearts of seventeenth-century people. The disease had no cure. And it killed one-third of the adults and more than half of the children it infected.*

Caused by the Variola *virus, smallpox has probably been present in human populations for about ten thousand years. The name of the virus comes from a Latin word that means "spotted" or "pimpled," in reference to the rash that appears on an afflicted person's skin.*

Inhaling the airborne virus from a smallpox victim's cough was all it took for the contagion to spread from person to person like wildfire. In nine to twelve days, an infected person fell ill with a headache, backache, diarrhea, fatigue, fever, and a raised red rash. Within several days, the rash turned into blister-like pustules that spread from the face to the chest, arms, and legs. In about nine days, the pustules broke open and scabs formed on the pits left behind. That's when most people died. For those who lived, the scabs dried and fell off, and the person's skin was left scarred with small, deep pits. Those who survived smallpox were immune to the disease for the rest of their lives.

Inoculation against smallpox was not practiced in England during the seventeenth century. The first professional inoculations in England and North America occurred in 1721. In 1796, Dr. Edward Jenner developed a smallpox vaccination. In 1979, the World Health Organization declared smallpox eradicated.

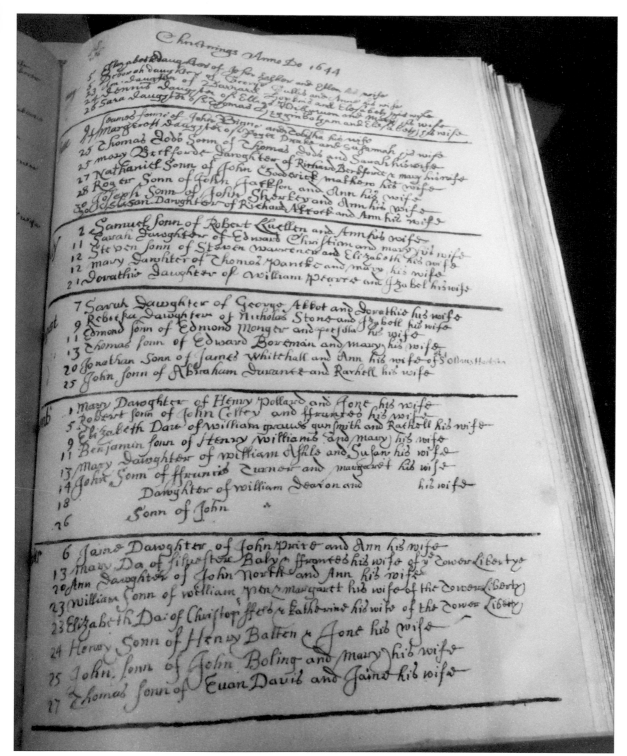

The baptism register in All Hallows by the Tower Church, London, records William Penn Jr.'s baptism, on October 23, 1644 (fifth line from the bottom).

The dawn of 1649 found King Charles I on trial for high treason, then sentenced to death. On January 30, 1649, an executioner beheaded him, and Oliver Cromwell assumed control of the government. If this upset William Penn Sr., he did not comment publicly. But young William certainly heard adults talk about the king's execution. Shortly afterward, William senior bought a country home outside of London.

When young William was about nine years old, he became a pupil at Chigwell School, several miles from his home. Chigwell, founded by the Anglican Church, was noted for its sound religious education, which favored neither Puritan nor Catholic practices. Considering the turbulent political climate — with Puritans, Anglicans, and Roman Catholics all vying for power — it was an educational choice above reproach.

In addition to grammar and mathematics, William Penn studied Latin and Greek and spoke both languages by the time he was eleven. But he especially enjoyed religion class and daily prayers. William later recalled that his first spiritual experience occurred when he was in his twelfth year and felt the presence of God as a brightening of the room and a sensation of inward peacefulness. Between the ages of twelve and fifteen, he experienced additional similar spiritual revelations. Later, as an adult, experiencing God in this way would become the very center of his religion.

Meanwhile, William senior's naval career soared. In a new war — this time against the Dutch — he became a national hero. In 1656, Cromwell granted him Macroom Castle, in Ireland, and presented him with a gold chain worth one hundred English pounds. Admiral William Penn was a very wealthy, very famous man.

Penn's career plummeted, however, when Cromwell, displeased with the results of a naval mission in the West Indies, ordered him jailed in

Because execution was a very real threat, political prisoners feared being sent to the Tower of London. The Penns' London home was within sight of the tower.

the Tower of London. To be nearer to her husband, Margaret moved the family back to Tower Hill Road. Once again, young William was living in the tower's shadow, but this time, his father's life was in jeopardy, as many of the tower's political prisoners were executed.

Fortunately, William senior's fame and the Royal Navy's high esteem weighed heavily in his favor, and Cromwell released him. Less than a year later, the Penn family moved to Macroom Castle, a decision with far-reaching consequences for young William.

A REBELLIOUS SON

The rambling estate of Macroom Castle was a far cry from their home in London. William was groomed for a public career and a place in society. His father taught him how to manage land and fight with a sword—accomplishments expected of a gentleman's son. A tutor brought from England educated young William in scholarly subjects.

William senior had, if not an open mind, at least a curious one. So, when Thomas Loe, a Quaker missionary, traveled to Ireland in 1657, William senior allowed him to hold a meeting in Macroom Castle. While preaching, Loe spoke about Inner Light and listening within oneself to hear God's voice. Loe's words resonated with listeners.

THE SOCIETY OF FRIENDS

*R*ADICAL AND OUTRAGEOUS—*that's what most English people thought of the Society of Friends, a religious group also known as the Quakers formed during the late 1640s. While still in his early twenties, George Fox, the group's founder, traveled the countryside conducting unstructured services. He spoke about understanding God through silent prayer, meditation, and reading the Bible. Quakers shunned the rituals and sacraments that were the backbone of the Anglican Church. There were no ordained clergy—no priests, no bishops. Instead, each Quaker received Inner Light or Truth through individual prayers made directly to God.*

Practicing peace, simplicity, and equality formed the core of Quaker beliefs. Quakers advocated plain living, including clothes free of fripperies such as lace and feather plumes. Believing all men to be equal, they did not acknowledge social class. They did not remove their hats to anyone, including royalty and government officials. When addressing a person, they used the words thee *and* thou *in lieu of formal titles. Quakers refused to fight in wars or to swear oaths. These practices, so contradictory to those of the Anglican Church, to British society, and in some cases to the requirements of British law, often led to arrest and imprisonment.*

William junior noticed that the family's black servant "could not contain himself from weeping aloud." When William looked at his father, he "saw the tears running down his cheeks." Loe's heartfelt words powerfully echoed young William's own spiritual revelations.

After Oliver Cromwell's death, in 1658, Parliament, pressured by a growing number of people who upheld the monarchy, invited Prince Charles (King Charles I's son) to return from exile in the Netherlands. In April 1660, thirty-one ships carrying loyal supporters sailed to the Netherlands to bring the exiled prince back to England. William senior was among those supporters. In appreciation, the prince, who shortly afterward was declared King Charles II, knighted William senior.

In 1660, young William was fifteen years old and headed to university, furthering his father's plans for an illustrious place in society. Sir William enrolled him at Christ Church college at Oxford University, one of England's most prestigious schools, long known for its support of the monarchy. With King Charles II on the throne, the social climate changed. Fancy clothing returned to fashion. England's theaters, which Oliver Cromwell had ordered closed, reopened. People once again attended plays and musical diversions. At Oxford, William found student parties and celebrations raucous and overwhelming. And he disagreed with worship practices of the Anglican Church, which the king had reinstated as England's official church. William preferred the company of students who shared his religious beliefs, rebellious beliefs that definitely did not conform to the strict rituals and boundaries of the Anglican Church.

On April 22, 1661, the two Williams, along with their neighbor (and famous diarist) Samuel Pepys, watched King Charles II and his retinue parade from the Tower of London to Whitehall Palace for the king's coronation. As Pepys described it, "Imbroidery and diamonds were ordinary among them. . . . The King, in a most rich imbrodered suit and cloak,

William Penn Jr., portrayed here at age twenty-two, began attending Quaker meetings in Ireland in 1666. Doing so changed the course of his life.

looked most nobly. . . . So glorious was the show with gold and silver, that we were not able to look at it—our eyes at last being so much overcome." And then "both the King and the Duke of Yorke took notice of us as he saw us at the window." Despite his preference for serious matters, imagine how sixteen-year-old William must have felt when the king and his younger brother, the Duke of York, nodded—maybe even waved—at him and his father.

Yet William Penn Jr. continued his rebellious religious path: "He, with certain other students of that University, withdrawing from the National Way of Worship, held Private Meetings for the Exercise of Religion, where they both preach'd and pray'd amongst themselves." This upset authorities, who fined the teenager for nonconformity.

William persisted in disregarding the university's disapproval. He attended meetings led by Dr. John Owen, a Puritan preacher and former head of Christ Church, even though he was no longer in the school's favor. Finally, the university expelled William for his unwillingness to conform to the boundaries set by the college and the church. Later, at the Penns' London home, a livid Sir William "endeavoured by both Words and Blows" to change his son's attitude. When William remained unmoved, his father angrily "turn'd him out of Doors."

The two Williams reconciled months later. Sir William sent young William to France, in the hope that the influence of French society would steer his wayward son back on a path within acceptable boundaries. While William enjoyed the frills of Paris—he appreciated fine clothes, fine food, and fine wine—he spent much of his time in the town of Saumur, where he studied with Moses Amyraut, a famous theologian known for his ideas about religious freedom. William returned to England in 1664. Samuel Pepys wryly noted that while William had acquired learning, he had also returned home with "a great deal, if not too much, of the vanity of the French garbe and affected manner of speech and gait—I fear all real profit he hath made of his travel will signify little." Perhaps Sir William found small comfort in the fact that his son, while still sober in religious practice, at least dressed fashionably.

For a short time, William studied law at Lincoln's Inn, the same place where George Calvert had studied. But, as preparations were under way for a new war against the Dutch, he left Lincoln's Inn and joined his father, who was back in command of the Royal Navy. During this time, William became better acquainted with the Duke of York, who, in addition to being the king's brother and the navy's lord high admiral, was Sir William's good friend. Occasionally, William acted as a courier between the duke and the king.

In 1666, occupied with the war, Sir William sent his son to Ireland to manage the estate at Macroom. While there, William attended Quaker meetings, finding himself increasingly in agreement with the sect's beliefs and practices—although he continued wearing fashionable clothes. Ironically, the Penns had received Macroom when Oliver Cromwell had stripped lands from Irish Catholics in retribution for the civil war. William knew the Quakers preached toleration. Did he ever consider that his family had benefited from political retaliation and religious persecution?

By autumn 1667, William had joined the Quakers. Shortly thereafter, he found his commitment to the group and its beliefs tested. At the end of a Quaker meeting, the authorities seized William and several other Quakers and threw them in jail. Their imprisonment was short, however, and by November William was back in England, where again he chafed at parental boundaries. Sir William vehemently disagreed with his son's religious choice, and the two Williams became estranged. William remained a Quaker, writing and preaching publicly about his beliefs. As a result, he was imprisoned three times during the years 1668 to 1671. The trial that led to his second imprisonment tested the boundaries of English law and became one of the most important court cases in England's history.

CRITICAL LEGAL BOUNDARIES

On August 14, 1670, several hundred Quakers, including William Penn and his friend William Mead, gathered for worship on Gracechurch Street, in London. Penn and Mead were arrested, but not for preaching. They were charged with attempting to incite a riot. An account of their trial stated that Penn and Mead did "Preach and Speak" in contempt of the king and of his law, thus disturbing and terrorizing many of the king's loyal subjects.

The trial began on September 3, 1670, with an eyebrow-raising exchange, not about rioting but about hats. A Quaker man never removed his hat when meeting someone. Doffing one's hat was a sign of subservience and, therefore, contrary to the Quaker belief in equality. When Penn and Mead entered the court, they were not wearing their hats. At the court's order, an official grabbed the men's hats and put them on their heads. When Penn stood in front of the judge, he was asked why he had not removed his hat, as was required as a sign of respect to the court. Adhering to Quaker beliefs, Penn answered, "Because I do not believe that to be any Respect." In response, the judge fined both Williams forty marks, a hefty sum of money, for "Contempt of the Court." To which Penn replied, "I desire it may be observed, that we came into the Court with our Hats off . . . and if they have been put on since, it was by Order from the Bench; and therefore not we, but the Bench [that] should be fined."

Penn refused to acknowledge the indictment for breaking the law, saying, "I desire you would let me know by what Law it is you Prosecute me, and upon what Law you ground my Indictment." He wasn't seeking a fight, but he knew that by not citing a specific law, the court was crossing a legal boundary. It was violating his legal right to know which law he had broken. When the court refused to specify, stating simply that he had violated "the Common-Law," Penn stated, "The Question is not whether I am Guilty . . . but whether this Indictment be Legal. It is too general and imperfect an Answer to say it is the Common-Law. . . . For where there is no Law, there is no Transgression."

Penn testified that the gathering on Gracechurch Street had been solely for worship and not to incite a riot. His testimony convinced the jury. They returned a verdict that Penn was guilty only of speaking on Gracechurch Street. And everyone knew that speaking was not a crime. The judge ordered the jury to reconsider its verdict, but it returned with the same decision. Angered, the judge told the jury:

> Gentlemen, you shall not be dismis[sed], till we have a Verdict that the Court will accept; and you shall be lock'd up, without Meat, Drink, Fire, and Tobacco: You shall not think thus to abuse the Court; we will have a [guilty] Verdict by the Help of God, or you shall starve for it.

As Penn pointed out, a jury's verdict "should be Free, and not Compelled." The judge had completely trampled the boundaries of English law, which guaranteed the right to a trial by jury. Before Penn was removed from the court, he spoke publicly to the jury: "You are Englishmen, mind your Priviledge, give not away your Right." Juror Edward Bushel replied, "Nor will we ever do it."

Bushel and the other jurors refused to change their verdict. The judge fined the members of the jury forty marks each and ordered them imprisoned until the fine was paid. Then he fined and imprisoned Penn and Mead for the only violation he could: contempt of court for not removing their hats at the beginning of the trial.

Penn intended to remain in prison with the jurors, but he received word that Sir William was ill and near death. Reluctantly, he allowed the payment of his fine so he could be at his dying father's bedside. Sir William died less than two weeks later. William junior was twenty-five years old.

While William grieved, the jury, still in jail, sued the judge of Penn's trial on the grounds that a jury had the right to decide a verdict without a judge's interference or coercion. A new judge ruled in their favor. This important right is one of the central foundations of law in the United States. Today, it is still a legal boundary that a judge cannot cross.

Chapter  Four

THE SEED OF A NATION

WILLIAM PENN continued to seek toleration for Quakers in England. In December 1670, he was arrested again. During his trial, he unhesitatingly defended the individual's right to worship free from government persecution, asserting that his preaching and writing were not illegal or harmful to either the government or the king. Even so, he was imprisoned in the Tower of London for six months. In 1674, he renewed his acquaintance with the Duke of York and for the first time in six years, returned to King Charles's court, where he lobbied against the persecution of Quakers. Meanwhile, militant Protestants had whipped the general public into anti-Catholic fervor, even casting doubts on the king's loyalty to England. They also cast doubts on those who associated with the king, including Penn. Because Quakers worshipped differently from members of the Anglican Church, they felt persecution's spillover effects. For several years, Quakers had been emigrating from England to America, especially to East and West Jersey, where they had purchased large land tracts. Penn found the idea of a land—a refuge—for Quakers appealing, and he approached King Charles II about establishing a colony in America.

In addition to being on good terms with the king and the Duke of York (who owned extensive properties in America), William had financial leverage that sweetened the pot. When Sir William was an admiral in the Royal Navy, he had loaned the king money for supplying the navy with food supplies at a time when the king's coffers were low. King Charles II owed Sir William sixteen thousand pounds, the debt still unpaid at Sir William's death, in 1670. In May 1680, young William petitioned the king for a colony in America. He secured the king's approval both by agreeing that the granting of the colony would settle the debt owed to his family and by presenting the grant as "a profitable plantation to the crown," much the way George Calvert had.

PENN'S CHARTER

On March 4, 1681, William Penn received King Charles II's royal charter for the colony of Pennsylvania. The charter stipulated that the colony was "to extend Westwards [from the Delaware River] five degrees in longitude . . . to be bounded on the North, by the beginning of the three and fortieth degree of Northern latitude, and on the south, by a circle drawne at twelve miles distance from [the town of] New Castle" and "by a straight line Westwards, to the limits of Longitude above mentioned" along the fortieth degree north parallel of latitude. The charter was very similar to the one King Charles I had given to George and Cecil Calvert. King Charles II named the colony Pennsylvania after his valued friend Sir William. (*Sylvania* means "forest land" in Latin.)

CURRENCY OF THE REALM

*I*N ENGLAND, *people pay for goods and services with monetary units called pounds, shillings, and pence. Until the twentieth century, one pound was equal to twenty shillings, and one shilling was equal to twelve pence (there were 240 pence to the pound). During the 1630s, it cost about 6,600 pounds to build an average warship for the Royal Navy.*

Pounds, shillings, and pence were also used in England's North American colonies. During the seventeenth and early eighteenth centuries, when these monies were scarce in the colonies, colonists most often settled bills by paying with valuable commodities produced in their colony. For example, Marylanders paid with tobacco, while other colonists used beaver skins or even wampum, a Native American form of currency consisting of shell beads threaded onto strings or woven into wide belts.

In the eighteenth century, each of England's colonies in North America began producing its own currency, still using the denominational names of pounds, shillings, and pence. Despite the similarity in names, however, a colonial pound could not be substituted one to one for an English pound, nor did one colony's pound equal that of another. To avoid confusion, an English pound was called a pound sterling. In 1764, a colonist shopping in Philadelphia for a pair of men's shoes made in England could expect to pay between eight and fifteen shillings a pair; a fine men's hat might cost thirty shillings.

In 1767, Maryland became the first American colony to issue paper currency in dollars. By royal decree, a colonial dollar was the equivalent of four shillings and six pence sterling.

This six-dollar bill was printed in Maryland in 1770. The reverse features images of strawberry and mint leaves, along with the phrase "Tis death to counterfeit."

Using his many contacts, especially those in the Quaker community, Penn quickly spread the word that land was for sale in Pennsylvania. He published a promotional tract that extolled his new province as a land of promise and targeted all potential immigrants, not just Quakers. In fact, Penn did not mention religion in the ad. Like George Calvert, William Penn—who was in debt—hoped that Pennsylvania's resources would bring him profit, so his ad emphasized the profits to be reaped from land, agricultural goods, and commerce. He sought not only people who could buy land but also those willing to rent, and even those willing to come as indentured servants, on terms similar to those offered by the Calverts in Maryland. As Penn wrote to a friend, he intended his province to be "the seed of a nation."

In August 1682, the Duke of York gave William two more deeds for an area called the Three Lower Counties (now the state of Delaware), located on the peninsula surrounded by Delaware Bay, Chesapeake Bay, and the Atlantic Ocean. A boundary line divided the Three Lower Counties from Maryland, which shared the peninsula. Charles Calvert—Cecil Calvert's son, the third Lord Baltimore and Maryland's governor—found his colony dwarfed by Penn's new land grants.

With plans under way for his own passage to the new colony, Penn wrote a letter stating his personal boundaries as the proprietor to the people who already lived there, so they would know what to expect:

> God has given me an understanding of my duty and an honest mind to do it uprightly. I hope you will not be troubled at your change and the king's choice. . . . You shall be governed by laws of your own making, and live a free and, if you will, a sober and industrious people. I shall not usurp the right of any, or oppress his person.

He sent agents to Pennsylvania with instructions to obtain land on the west bank of the Delaware River for the province's capital city, to be named Philadelphia, from two Greek words that mean "brotherly love." He also instructed his agents to buy large tracts of land from the Lenni-Lenape (called Delaware Indians by the English) who lived in the region.

Penn emphasized his ideal of a colony that welcomed and tolerated diverse peoples. In October 1681, his passage to the colony delayed, he sent a separate letter to the Lenni-Lenape. In this letter, William acknowledged that European colonists had treated Indians with unkindness and injustice. He wrote that he regretted the animosities between Indians and colonists and the bloodshed that had occurred, and he assured the Indians that he held them in high regard and intended nothing but peace and friendship. He also wrote that just as he expected fair, equal treatment for himself in British courts, he intended similar justice for all of Pennsylvania's inhabitants, Indians and colonists alike.

ABOARD THE WELCOME

Penn boarded the ship *Welcome* for Pennsylvania on August 29, 1682. Although he was excited to visit his new colony, he left England with mixed feelings. Earlier that year his mother, Margaret, had passed away, and he was leaving his wife, Gulielma, and their two sons and daughter behind. Just weeks before the *Welcome* sailed, he sent them a letter that ended, "So farewell to my thrice dearly beloved wife and children. Yours, as God pleases, in that which no waters can quench, no time forget, nor distance wear away, but remains forever." It would be months, if not years, until he would see them again. Yet his family was always in his mind. Letters to each of his children were among the last he wrote before the ship sailed.

Storms and pirates were only two of the potential hazards that passengers on the *Welcome* faced. Serious injury and illness were equally hazardous due to limited medical care while at sea. News that a smallpox

INVISIBLE LINES

*P*INPOINTING A LOCATION *on the earth's surface is made easy using a grid of lines called the parallels of latitude and the meridians of longitude. Parallels of latitude encircle the earth horizontally. Meridians of longitude encircle the earth vertically, through the North and South Poles, and intersect parallels of latitude perpendicularly.*

Lines of latitude and longitude are measured in degrees. Because each line completely encircles the earth, it measures 360 degrees. Lines of latitude and longitude are further divided into minutes and seconds — 60 minutes equals one degree, and 60 seconds equals one minute. The equator, at zero degrees latitude, divides the earth into the Northern and Southern Hemispheres. All other parallels of latitude are written in a way that indicates how many degrees north or south of the equator they are located. Traveling north from the equator, you would eventually reach the North Pole, at a point called 90 degrees north (90° N). In the same manner, traveling south, you would eventually reach the South Pole, at 90 degrees south (90° S). Since there is no meridian of longitude comparable to the equator, mapmakers use the meridian along which Greenwich, England, lies as zero degrees longitude. This meridian is called the prime meridian. Each meridian of longitude is noted as being up to 180 degrees east or 180 degrees west of the prime meridian. Both latitude and longitude must be included to identify a specific location. Philadelphia is 39°57' N/75°9' W.

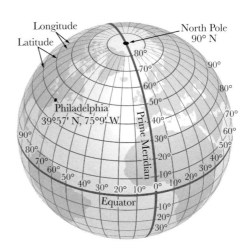

epidemic had broken out on the ship terrified the colonists. In the following weeks, the disease killed thirty-one people — almost one-third of the *Welcome's* passengers. Penn, who had survived the disease at age three, was immune. Fellow passenger Richard Townsend later wrote that Penn showed compassion for the sick and helped meet their needs with care.

The *Welcome* sailed into Delaware Bay on October 24. Almost at once, Penn invited the Duke of York's agents to a meeting on board the ship. During the meeting, he showed them the deeds signed and sealed by the duke. Later, the agents relinquished control of the Three Lower Counties to him, symbolically presenting the land to him with a key to the fort at New Castle, a chunk of turf with a twig on it, and a bowl filled with river water and soil.

Penn disembarked from the *Welcome* and traveled up the Delaware River, first landing in the town of Upland (now Chester) and then moving on to Shackamaxon, just north of the site chosen for Philadelphia. He attended a whirlwind of political and religious meetings during the following months. He met with colonists—Quakers, Anglicans, Swedes, and Dutch—and set up the provincial government. Penn's legislative

To better understand the issues of his colony, William Penn invited representatives from many different communities to attend a provincial conference.

In 1682, the Lenni-Lenape presented this wampum belt to William Penn as they discussed a treaty. The belt indicated that a very serious matter was under discussion.

assembly included many Quakers, but he also extended representation to non-Quakers living in the Three Lower Counties. By the end of 1683, Penn had purchased large tracts of land along the west bank of the Delaware River from the Lenni-Lenape. A treaty between Penn and the Lenni-Lenape contained language to establish an honest, peaceful relationship that respected the boundaries of each culture. Both parties expressed hopes that future relations, particularly in the fur trade, would prove profitable for all.

In 1680, fewer than seven hundred people of European descent lived in Pennsylvania. After Penn received the charter, European immigrants flocked to the region. Its growing economy demanded an increased workforce. As in Maryland, indentured servants were commonplace. Hypocritically, even as the large Quaker population preached equality, some wealthy Quakers in Pennsylvania owned African and African-American slaves.

Twenty-three immigrant-filled ships sailed from England to Pennsylvania during 1681 and 1682. By Penn's estimate, in July 1683 "about 80 houses are built [in Philadelphia], and . . . above 300 farms settled" in the surrounding area. The colony flourished. Yet one provincial issue continually plagued Penn: the boundary line between Pennsylvania and Maryland. Whether discussions were by letter or face-to-face, he and Charles Calvert could not agree on where the boundary fell.

Chapter  Five

WHOSE LAND?

EVEN THOUGH forty-nine years had passed since George Calvert had received his charter, the exact location of the fortieth degree north parallel of latitude remained unknown. This vagueness had not, however, prevented Kings Charles I and II from using the parallel to establish a more-than-two-hundred-mile-long boundary line. When the Calverts had first settled in Maryland, this wasn't a problem: there was a lot of land and few colonists. By 1681, the situation had changed. A steady stream of new settlers established homesteads in the wilderness areas of both colonies, even in places where the boundary line was unclear. Both William Penn and Charles Calvert authorized land grants according to their perceptions of the line's location. The colonists who bought these lands in good faith felt the squeeze when officials from both provinces requested tax payments. And each colony had its own laws and regulations. Which colony's laws should the colonists living in the border area follow? The stage was set for some spectacular feuds.

The two lords proprietors expressed boundary concerns as early as April 10, 1681, when William Penn wrote to Charles Calvert. Writing he was a "strainger in the affaires of the Country," Penn asked Calvert to give Penn's representative all the help he could with regard to "the business of the bounds" and "observing our just limitts" so they could have a "Just & friendly" relationship.

Five months later, Penn wrote to six prominent planters who lived in the counties that bordered the northern reach of Chesapeake Bay. In preparing the letter, Penn consulted a map he had published and distributed — on which he had erroneously placed the fortieth parallel about fifty miles too far south, to include the city of Baltimore. Penn's letter cautioned the planters that as they lived within what he believed were the boundaries of Pennsylvania, none of them ought to "pay any more taxes or assessments by any order or law of Maryland." This news upset the planters, who unquestionably identified themselves as Marylanders. But some of them obeyed Penn's order and stopped paying taxes to Maryland. This threat to property and income alarmed and angered Charles Calvert. Meetings among provincial representatives and letters sent to various officials left the situation unresolved.

In December 1682, Penn traveled to Maryland, where he and Calvert met for the first time. Penn had realized that his interpretation of the boundary line was incorrect, but as no one knew by what amount, he wasn't ready to give up. In order to export Pennsylvania's resources overseas, he needed direct access to major waterways. Trade would be severely restricted without Chesapeake Bay and the mouth of the Susquehanna River under his control, so Penn offered to buy some of that land from Calvert. The meeting ended with no resolution other than a promise to meet again sometime in 1683.

LOSS, DEATHS, AND HEIRS

In the following years, matters only got worse. Citing confusion over the definition of "unsettled land," Calvert claimed that per the charter granted his family by King Charles I, the Three Lower Counties belonged to him. In 1684, concerned about the feud's outcome, Penn returned to England, where he could better defend his legal right to ownership. Calvert soon did likewise.

Despite the Decree of 1685, an act by the British Board of Trade and Foreign Plantations that attempted to settle the boundary issues, dissension continued for decades. In 1689, after a revolution in England, the royal charter for Maryland was withdrawn from Charles Calvert. England's new king, William III, took control of the colony. The boundary issue did not improve in the early 1700s. After Calvert died, in 1715, his son and heir, Benedict, the fourth Lord Baltimore, renounced Roman Catholicism, joined the Anglican Church, and petitioned King William, a Protestant, for the return of the Maryland charter. Benedict died two months after his father, so did not live to see his petition granted. But the king did restore the charter for Maryland to Benedict's son, fifteen-year-old Charles, who became the fifth Lord Baltimore. Born in England, this new Charles, grandson of the first Charles Calvert, had never seen Maryland.

Meanwhile, William Penn, severely in debt, unsuccessfully attempted to sell Pennsylvania back to the crown. He suffered a mild stroke in 1712; a second and then a third, yet more severe, stroke followed within the next year. Subsequently weak and incapacitated, William slowly declined and passed away in 1718.

In 1732, Charles Calvert, fifth Lord Baltimore, met in England with William Penn's sons Richard, John, and Thomas, the new proprietors of Pennsylvania. The four men signed an agreement for a formal survey of the boundary lines. The survey would essentially follow the boundary lines as outlined in the Decree of 1685. The peninsula containing the Three Lower Counties would be divided in half equally by a north-south boundary that extended south to Cape Henlopen. The northern boundary of the Three Lower Counties was defined by a circle with a twelve-mile radius centered on New Castle, though the precise center point was still undetermined. The northern boundary of Maryland, formerly defined as lying along the latitude 40 degrees north, would now be defined as lying along the parallel of latitude that lay fifteen miles south of Philadelphia. When he signed the 1732 agreement, Charles Calvert, who was unfamiliar with the territory until he visited Maryland later that year, mistakenly ceded to the Penns all the territory that their father, William, had claimed back in 1681 — nearly two thousand square miles. Charles was not happy when he discovered his error.

Despite the agreement, no formal survey took place. Maryland officials continually enticed colonists to settle in uncertain territory as Marylanders. Consequently, mistaken perceptions of land ownership led to ongoing disputes between Maryland and Pennsylvania colonists who lived near the boundary lines in question. Two Pennsylvanian officials, John Wright and Samuel Blunston, expressed their confusion in a letter to Pennsylvania's governor, Patrick Gordon:

> But as the Line between the two Provinces was not Known, no Authority was claimed over those few Families settled . . . by or under Pretence of Maryland Rights, but they remained (by us) undisturbed, tho' many Inhabitants of Pennsylvania lived some Miles to the Southward of them.

Settlers and officials were baffled. And still the Penns and Lord Baltimore dragged their feet.

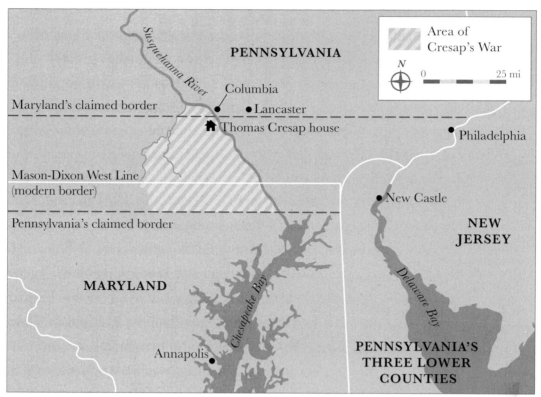

Unclear boundaries led to conflict and even violence. The most infamous dispute became known as Cresap's War. White lines represent modern state boundaries.

HORSES AND A HEFTY REWARD

The most infamous boundary dispute was the long-running battle between Marylander Thomas Cresap and his Pennsylvanian neighbors. When Cresap arrived in Maryland as a teenager in about 1717, he intended to buy land. Unfortunately, his debts piled up faster than his riches. To escape his debts, Cresap fled to Virginia, where he got married and lived on a rented farm. By 1729, the Cresaps had returned to Maryland and, considering themselves Marylanders, purchased land along the Susquehanna River. Their homestead lay along the 40 degrees north line of latitude, near modern-day Columbia, about eighty miles west of Philadelphia. Cresap couldn't have picked a more troublesome spot.

Cresap's boundary trouble started with horses. Pennsylvanian-owned horses knocked down Marylanders' fences and trampled their corn. More trouble occurred when three Pennsylvanians boarded Cresap's ferry and, midway across the Susquehanna River, drew their guns on Cresap. As Cresap pulled in his oar, one of the men hit him with a gun and threw him overboard. Cresap swam to an island, from which he was later rescued. In his formal complaint, Cresap declared himself a Marylander and a tenant of Lord Baltimore. Later testimony would reveal that the Pennsylvanians actually had an issue with Cresap's workman, but the dispute played into ongoing boundary-line tensions.

In 1732, Pennsylvanians alleged that Cresap and the Maryland militia had burned the homes of friendly Indians and unlawfully imprisoned them. When Pennsylvania's governor complained, Maryland's governor simply informed Cresap that "so long as he behaves himself well, he shall be protected from any Insults of the Pennsylvanians; and that it is the best Method for him to live in Peace and Friendship with the Indians."

Thomas Cresap carried people and livestock across the Susquehanna River on a ferry similar to this one.

Later that year, Pennsylvania traders claimed Marylanders killed several of their packhorses. One man testified that Cresap had admitted to him that he had done the killing because "he lived in the Jurisdiction of Maryland, and that said [Pennsylvanian] horses had no right to be there."

In retaliation for the incident, a group of Pennsylvanians rode to Marylander John Lowe's home and accused him of killing their horses. They dragged Lowe onto the frozen Susquehanna River, saying he would be brought to justice in the Province of Pennsylvania. Eyewitness Cresap shouted, "If the Lord Baltimore would not Protect them in their Rights and land, They the [Maryland] Inhabitants . . . must apply to the King." Cresap testified that a Pennsylvanian replied that "they have no Business with the King nor the King with them for Penn was their King."

An angry Lord Baltimore issued a proclamation charging ten men, all of whom were allegedly "being or pretending to be Inhabitants of Pensylvania," with storming Lowe's plantation in a "Riotous manner Armed with Offensive and Defensive Weapons," beating Lowe, his wife, and his children, and imprisoning Lowe and his sons. Lord Baltimore offered a reward of "Ten pounds Current Money of this our Province" for each man who was caught and convicted.

CRESAP'S WAR

Unbelievably, the situation worsened. On January 29, 1733, Cresap's wife, Hannah, and a group of Cresap's tenant farmers were preparing logs to build a house and a boat. Mounted Pennsylvanian officials arrived at the site—one of the land parcels under boundary dispute—and arrested eight of Cresap's workers. Her horse at a gallop, Hannah raced home to warn her husband.

At seven o'clock that evening, hoofbeats approached the Cresaps' house. Worried, the Cresaps and seven or eight friends barricaded the door with benches. Two men knocked and requested a place to sleep. Cresap refused and threatened to shoot if they didn't leave. The men replied that they had come to arrest him. Pennsylvanian Knoles Daunt tried to force open the door. Cresap poked the barrel of his gun under the bottom of the door and pulled the trigger, wounding Daunt. The Pennsylvanians fled, carrying Daunt with them. He died several days later.

Pennsylvania's governor insisted that Cresap be tried for murder. However, the trial was held in a Maryland court. The jury concluded that Cresap, provoked and fearful for the safety of his family, had been justified in his action and was therefore acquitted.

And still the trouble escalated. In March 1735, Cresap testified that he had reliable information that Pennsylvanian officials "have offered large Rewards to several Persons to take this Deponent [Cresap] either dead or alive, and to set his . . . house on fire."

A few months later, John Wright, a Pennsylvanian justice of the peace, stated that Cresap "came with about twenty Persons, Men, Women & Lads, armed with Guns, Swords & Pistols & Blunderbusses & Drum beating" to his land while he was peaceably harvesting his wheat. Wright swore that Cresap and his group had brought empty wagons with the intention of stealing the grain from his field.

The powder keg between Cresap and the Pennsylvanians exploded on November 23, 1736. As midnight approached, Samuel Smith, the sheriff of Lancaster County, and twenty-four Pennsylvanians "armed with guns, pistols, and swords" surrounded Cresap's home. The sheriff read out a warrant for Cresap's arrest, charging him with the murder of Knoles Daunt and various other "high Crimes & Misdemeanors" against Pennsylvanians. The sheriff demanded his surrender, saying that "they would not depart . . . until they had [Cresap] dead or alive." The Pennsylvanian posse reported that in response to their declaration, Cresap cussed, called the people of Pennsylvania "Quakeing Dogs & Rogues," and vowed to fight rather than surrender. According to Cresap, his terrified wife, Hannah, "who was very big with child . . . fell in Labor with the Fright."

Much of the next day, shouts and shots peppered the air. Finally, the Pennsylvanians tossed firebrands onto Cresap's roof. Fearing his family would be burned alive, Cresap insisted that Hannah—still in labor—and the children leave while he and the men remained behind. Flames soon engulfed the house, forcing Cresap and the other men out. More gunfire left one man dead and two men, including Cresap, wounded.

Under arrest and surrounded by angry officials, Cresap taunted his captors. As they entered the city of Philadelphia, he turned to a member of the posse and said, "This is one of the Prettyest Towns in Maryland." Cresap was more correct than the furious posse knew. Philadelphia, at latitude 39°57' N, is south of the fortieth parallel. According to Lord Baltimore's royal charter, the city was in Maryland.

Cresap remained in jail for several months. After his release, he moved farther west, where he continued to play an important role in the European settlement of Maryland.

THE COURT DECIDES

Although everyone clamored for clarity, nothing concrete was done to resolve the boundary-line issues. In 1735, King George II, disgusted with the situation, ordered England's Court of Chancery, which handled cases regarding property and land, to settle the matter. Even as the case dragged on, the two provinces awarded new land grants in disputed territories despite the king's order against it. They further ignored the king's command that "the Governors of the respective Provinces of Maryland & Pensylvania . . . Do not upon pain of incurring his Majestys highest Displeasure permit or Suffer any Tumults, Riots, or other Outrageous Disorders to be Committed on the Borders of their respective Provinces." Exasperated, Pennsylvania's governor, Patrick Gordon, commented to Maryland's governor, Samuel Ogle, "Nothing is more certain, than that the two Provinces, what ever Jangling there may be about it, must necessarily bound on each other, & have some Limits fixed, unless we are perpetually to quarrell."

Finally, in 1750, fifteen years after the case—which had become known as the Great Chancery Suit—was filed, Lord Justice Hardwicke declared a verdict. The boundaries as outlined in the 1732 agreement would stand. The Penns and Charles Calvert had no choice but to agree. Each province appointed several men to a joint boundary-line commission.

As a group, the boundary commissioners agreed that the belfry of the courthouse in New Castle would be the center point for the circle with the twelve-mile radius to be drawn around that city. The commissioners hired local surveyors (some from each colony) and supplied them with instructions and provisions. They directed the surveyors to report their progress to the commissioners regularly. Commissioners from both provinces attended meetings, sometimes at specific sites on the line when disputes over placement arose and sometimes when boundary stones were being placed, to make sure their respective provinces did not get cheated.

SERVING ON THE BOUNDARY COMMISSION

*T*HE LORDS PROPRIETORS *commissioned, in writing, seven men from each province to serve as their representatives during the boundary-line survey. These commissioners directed the surveyors hired to run the boundary line and managed the logistics of purchasing supplies and paying the survey crew. The first group of commissioners met on October 17, 1732. It wasn't long before they disagreed. They disagreed about the location of the center of the circle around New Castle. They disagreed about whether King Charles II's charter for William Penn had intended a circle with a twelve-mile radius or a twelve-mile circumference (the latter would mean more land for Pennsylvania). The arguments ended in a stalemate. (A court later ruled that the twelve-mile reference was to the circle's radius.)*

Over time, new commissioners replaced old as vacancies due to illness, even death, required. In 1750, Benjamin Chew, a Philadelphia lawyer who was born in Maryland, was appointed secretary of the commission. He held the position for many years, and at times it sorely tried his patience. Survey crews crossing farmland often caused damage—enough so that in December 1760, the commissioners ordered the surveyors to obtain the consent of property owners before traipsing through orchards and gardens. Furthermore, they decreed, cutting down fruit trees to clear a vista, or line of view for the survey line, was not allowed without the landowner's permission.

When commissioners attended boundary-line meetings, the lords proprietors paid for their travel, lodging, and meals. As men of high standing in their communities—landowners, clergymen, provincial officials, lawyers, and a professor—the commissioners stayed at inns and ate meals that met their standard of living. Expense accounts for the 1760 survey included such items as candles, Madeira wine, a teakettle, tea, chocolate, sugar, a Cheshire cheese, and rum. At times, one or more commissioners who had surveying experience actually worked as part of the survey crew and supervised portions of the line, such as setting boundary stone markers. But most often they met with the crew at inns for progress updates. Since the boundary commissioners served for a specified length of time, their commissions had to be periodically "enlarged," meaning renewed. The commissioners did receive payment for their services.

FAILED ATTEMPTS

In April 1751, colonial surveyors began running a line from Fenwick Island, on the Atlantic coast, straight west across the Delaware peninsula to Chesapeake Bay. They marked the start of the line, near the shoreline, with a crown stone made of local rock. The crown stone was carved with the Calvert coat of arms facing south and the Penn coat of arms facing north. The survey crew placed additional crown stones at five-mile intervals for the next twenty miles and wooden posts at every mile in between. (Within ten years, the first crown stone was found overturned, lying on the ground. Maryland Commissioner J. Beale Bordley reported a rumor that vandals digging for pirate loot were responsible.)

By May, the crew was mired in mud deep within the Pocomoke Swamp. (*Pocomoke* is an Algonquian word that means "black water.") The crew waded around cypress knees and pushed aside clingy tangles of aquatic plants. They warded off snakes and snapping turtles, scratched itchy insect bites, and pulled off sucking leeches. The closest dry ground where they could pitch their tents was a two-mile hike away. Fed up, the disgruntled men went on strike. In a journal entry for May 8, 1751, John Emory and Thomas Jones, the surveyors and bosses, wrote, "This morning our Workmen combined together to Exhort higher Wages from us and . . . [would not] work longer with us unless we would enlarge their wages." Threats to the strike leaders and discussion with the rest of the men resulted in all returning to work with no pay raise. The men continued under grueling conditions working "till late at night often to the mid-thigh in water." In fact, water so inundated the exact spot where the twenty-five-mile marker was to be placed the crew couldn't set the sixth (and last) crown stone.

Instead they marked the line's halfway point — dubbing it the Middle Point — with another crown stone. Despite nasty conditions, the crew completed the job, marking a straight line across the peninsula, a distance of almost seventy miles. But that only provided the peninsula's southern boundary line between Maryland and Pennsylvania.

Between 1760 and 1763, another team of surveyors attempted several times to run the peninsula's eighty-mile-long eastern boundary line, referred to as the Tangent Line. By the terms of the Chancery Suit, the Tangent Line was to extend northward from the Middle Point until it reached a point tangent to, or touching, the circle drawn around New Castle. If the line had run straight north along the meridian, it would have been much easier. Instead, to reach the tangent point from the Middle Point, the Tangent Line had to run at an angle of 3 degrees 32 minutes 5 seconds northwest from the Middle Point. That made the survey a lot harder — maybe even impossible. Imagine trying to draw a straight line from your home to the doorway of one specific building located eighty miles away with no reference points in between to guide your direction. That's a bit what running the Tangent Line was like.

The surveyors' northwestward trek from the Middle Point was fine for the first few miles. By June 16, 1762, conditions must have deteriorated, since Pennsylvania surveyor John Lukens wrote to Pennsylvania commissioner Richard Peters to inform him that he was aware of errors between his attempt at running the Tangent Line and earlier attempts. Frustrated, Lukens ended his letter, "I pray to be released from Trying to Do what I now Conceive to be Impossible, Viz. Run a Straight Line of ye Lenth of 80 miles." His crew struggled on. At the end of August, Lukens informed Peters that navigating uneven, swampy areas near the Choptank River had greatly delayed his crew and caused them to have to make "three different offsets of the line." (Under the instruction of the boundary commission, Lukens and his crew were to stop if they found the Tangent Line off course by more than ten feet for every five miles.) Optimistically, Lukens concluded the note with his hope that his crew would finish the Tangent Line within ten days to two weeks.

Unfortunately, by the time they reached the area where they expected to find the tangent point (the spot where the Tangent Line touched the circle drawn around New Castle), the line was too far east. The surveyors made yet another attempt during the summer of 1763. That line ended up 346½ feet too far west. The surveyors' attempts had failed. Boundary bickering continued. And everyone wondered if the trouble would ever end.

Chapter Six

STARS IN THEIR EYES

FREDERICK CALVERT (the sixth and latest Lord Baltimore) and William Penn's sons Richard and Thomas (John died in 1746) were as fed up with boundary-line hooliganism as the colonists were. Then they heard about Charles Mason and Jeremiah Dixon, two men who had scientists buzzing about their recent success with important astronomical observations. Glowing reports about the pair's precise observations of the transit of Venus, as well as additional celestial observations they had made in South Africa, had traveled through the scientific community. And what was more, Dixon's surveying skills were equally lauded. If any two men could use the stars to direct long survey lines across uncertain colonial territories, it was these two.

Having an experienced astronomer as one of the Maryland-Pennsylvania boundary surveyors would be critical. Plotting the boundary lines' directions would require locating the specific positions of stars at precise times during the night. The coordinates of the stars' positions, when mathematically triangulated with the surveyors' instruments, could be used to pinpoint locations on the earth's surface.

THE STARS IN YOUR SKY

*C*OLONIAL NAVIGATORS *looked to the night sky and the celestial sphere as they sailed the Atlantic Ocean to the New World. The word* celestial *comes from the Latin word* caelestis, *meaning "sky" or "heaven." The celestial sphere completely surrounds Earth. Imagine Earth as a ball inside an infinitely larger ball. Now, mentally push Earth's equator straight out into space, and it becomes a celestial equator that divides the celestial sphere into the northern and southern skies. A meridian, a north-south line, is another imaginary celestial line that astronomers and navigators use. A meridian is a line that encircles the celestial sphere in a north-south manner and crosses through the zenith, a point directly above any location. For example, someone in Philadelphia looks up and sees a zenith specific to his or her location and therefore would establish a specific meridian based on it, while someone in London would have his or her own zenith and meridian.*

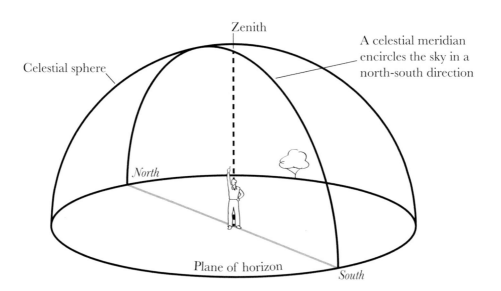

Since the earth beneath your feet prevents you from seeing the half of the celestial sphere on the opposite side of the planet, your view of the celestial sphere is never more than half. And your horizon always limits your view of the stars.

For countless centuries, people have grouped certain stars into constellations that remind them of figures, real and mythological. There are eighty-eight officially recognized constellations: twenty-eight in the northern sky, forty-eight in the southern sky, and twelve in the swatch of the sky that lies within the path that the sun appears to travel during the course of a year. The sun's apparent path is called the ecliptic. (The constellations in this path are called the zodiac.) Constellations are named after animals or mythological heroes, such as Cygnus the Swan and Orion the hunter. Constellations always remain in the same positions relative to one another.

During the course of a night, constellations seem to travel slowly westward across the sky. In reality, it's you moving as the earth rotates daily on its axis from west to east.

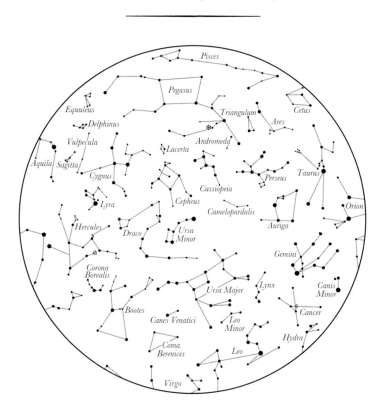

These are the constellations visible in the Northern Hemisphere. The specific ones you can see when you look at the sky depend on your location and the season.

Mathematician and astronomer Charles Mason, born in 1728, knew the night sky as well as he knew his own neighborhood. As a boy growing up in Sapperton, England, Mason greatly preferred calculating the locations of stars to helping his father mill wheat and bake bread. At that time, Robert Stratford, a local mathematician who served as the village schoolmaster, generously encouraged Mason's love of mathematics and taught him the math skills he would need to become an astronomer. In 1756, Charles Mason, who was by then married and had two sons, joined the staff of the Royal Observatory at Greenwich, England.

Jeremiah Dixon was born in Bishop Auckland, England, on July 27, 1733. His father was a Quaker and the owner of a coal mine. As with Mason, mathematics and astronomy interested Dixon from an early age. John Bird, a famous maker of mathematical and astronomical instruments, also lived in Bishop Auckland and was one of Dixon's friends and mentors. Dixon studied surveying and was a skilled draftsman. According to family legend, Dixon often wore a long red coat and a three-cornered hat. If this was true, he certainly world have cut a striking figure striding across the countryside with his surveyor's equipment.

THE TRANSIT OF VENUS

Mason and Dixon made newspaper headlines in 1760, when the Royal Society in London, a scientific academy of distinguished scientists, hired them to observe an astronomical event called the transit of Venus. Periodically, the orbital path of a celestial body — a planet, for example — carries it in front of a larger one. During the transit of Venus, the planet Venus passes between Earth and the sun. While doing so, it appears as a black dot moving across the surface of the sun. The Royal

Society wanted the transit observed and recorded because astronomical data collected during the transit would enable them to calculate the distance between the earth and the sun. From that, they could calculate the size of our solar system. But a transit of Venus is a very rare event. It happens only twice in a century. And one would occur in 1761.

Being chosen for the mission was a tremendous honor. Thirty-two-year-old Mason and twenty-seven-year-old Dixon eagerly accepted the job of tracking and timing Venus's path across the solar disk. Since the sun must be visible to see this event, nighttime observation is impossible. In some locations, the entire transit can be seen. In others, depending on when sunrise and sunset occur, only part of the transit is visible. Mason and Dixon's commission was to observe the entire transit. The Royal Society decided that the best place for them to do that was on Sumatra, one of the Indonesian islands in the Indian Ocean. Sea travel during the 1700s was a serious undertaking, yet the adventurous astronomers willingly risked danger in their quest for new scientific information. To arrive in time for the June 1761 transit, the Royal Society advised them to leave England six to seven months beforehand.

Attack!

Making arrangements for the trip took time. Mason and Dixon gently packed delicate astronomical instruments, cushioning them against the rigors of sea travel. Since Mason's wife, Rebecca, had died the previous year, he arranged long-term child care for his sons, Doctor Isaac and William. The possibility that Mason would never see them again was very real.

By November 1760, the *Seahorse*, a twenty-four-gun ship in England's Royal Navy, was ready to leave for Bencoolen, a British military post on

MORE INVISIBLE LINES

*L*ATITUDE AND LONGITUDE *were critical lines for Mason and Dixon's work, as were another set of invisible lines. This other set of lines is located on the celestial sphere.*

A star's altitude is its angular distance above the horizon relative to the person observing the star. But knowing only a star's altitude wouldn't help an observer in a different area locate the star. So astronomers divided the celestial sphere into a grid of lines, similar to the latitude and longitude lines used by mapmakers. Each star is assigned two coordinates that pinpoint its location on the celestial sphere. People anywhere on Earth can locate a star once they know these coordinates, known as right ascension and declination. (Note that while the celestial meridian, discussed on page 54, is subjective—dependent on one's location—right ascension and declination are set grids, like longitude and latitude.)

When Mason and Dixon observed a star, they always recorded its right ascension. Right ascension is like a meridian of longitude, except it's a point on the celestial sphere rather than on Earth's surface. A star's right ascension is determined by measuring its position along the celestial equator. Its location is measured as an angular distance, a portion of the 360 degrees that make the full circle of the celestial equator. Instead of starting at the prime meridian, as is done with longitude, the starting point for right ascension begins at the vernal, or spring, equinox. The vernal equinox occurs on or about March 21, when the sun's position in the sky begins to move from south to north across the celestial equator. That point on the celestial sphere is considered zero degrees. Moving from east to west, right ascension is measured in hours, minutes, and seconds along the celestial equator. The hours increase from zero to twenty-four—the number of hours it takes Earth to rotate completely on its axis once. Each hour is equal to an angle of fifteen degrees. (15 × 24 = 360, the number of degrees in a circle.) When looking at Earth, it helps to think of right ascension as divisional lines, or coordinates, that go from left to right.

The other imaginary celestial grid line is a star's declination, which is similar to a parallel of latitude. A star's declination is its angular distance north or south of the celestial equator. Declination is measured in degrees, minutes, and seconds. The celestial equator has a declination of zero degrees. The celestial north pole is expressed as +90°; the celestial south pole is −90°. Mason carried a star table, given to him by the Royal Society, that listed the declinations of all the stars he and Dixon would see.

Antares is the brightest star in the zodiac constellation Scorpius. Mason and Dixon often observed Antares while they were in Africa. Antares's coordinates are: right ascension 16 hours 29 minutes 24 seconds, declination −26 degrees 25 minutes 55 seconds. The minus sign in the declination lets the observer know that the star is located south of the celestial equator.

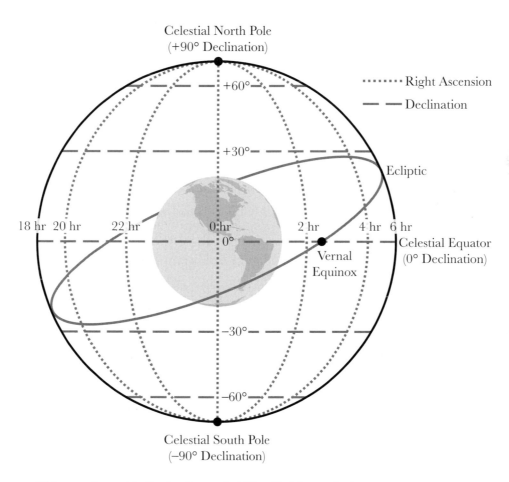

Right ascension and declination form an invisible grid of lines and points on the celestial sphere, similar to longitude and latitude on the earth's surface.

Sumatra. Mason and Dixon were ready, too. "We wait for nothing but a fair wind," they wrote. But business snafus prevented the surveyors (and the *Seahorse*'s impatient captain) from departing until January 8. Less than forty-eight hours after they set sail, a crewman sounded an alert: a French warship was approaching. Cannonballs flying toward the *Seahorse* chased thoughts of Venus from Mason's and Dixon's minds.

The cannon fire lasted for more than an hour. Shaken, Dixon reported news of the attack to the secretary of the Royal Society: "Our loss amounts to 11 killed and 37 wounded, (a great many of which are mortal) our Riging and Masts are very much damaged being rendered quite unfit for service, and her Hull much wounded."

Dixon and Mason worried that repairs would "take up so much time that it will be impossible for us to reach India soon enough to make the Observations upon the Transit." They suggested the Royal Society consider a closer place for their observation. The society threatened them with legal action if they didn't resume travel as planned. So Dixon and Mason waited while carpenters repaired the *Seahorse*.

BLACK DOT ON THE SUN

Once travel resumed, it became clear that the ship could not reach Sumatra in time for the transit of Venus. Mason and Dixon disembarked at the Cape of Good Hope, South Africa, at the end of April 1761. There they paid the *Seahorse*'s carpenters to build a circular observatory, from which they would observe the transit. Bricks provided a level floor. A conical roof capped the observatory's five-and-a-half-foot-tall canvas wall with an opening "easily turned to any part of the heavens." To shield the instruments from wind and weather, the carpenters tarred the top of the observatory and filled the joints with putty.

Mason and Dixon's observatory at the Cape of Good Hope was constructed of canvas, wood, and bricks and did more than just shelter their instruments. It also provided them with a stable base from which to make their observations and measurements. The observatory pictured here is similar to the one they built.

A pendulum clock affixed in a wooden case was crucial for Mason and Dixon's astronomical observations. To assure accuracy, it had to be absolutely level on top of an unshakable, immovable base. The carpenters set the base's wooden posts four feet deep in the ground. With the clock wound and ready to go, each swing of the pendulum brought June 5, the date of the transit, closer.

At last the big event began. Mason and Dixon observed the transit with two telescopes and an astronomical instrument called a Hadley's quadrant, which is used to measure angles. They recorded the time when Venus first touched the outer rim of the solar disk and the moment when it became visible on the solar disk as a complete black dot. They also recorded Venus's exit off the disk—when it first touched the other edge of the solar disk and the moment when it completely passed off the solar disk.

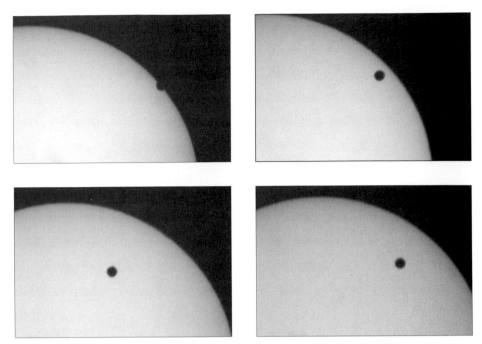

The most recent transit of Venus occurred in June 2012. As the transit progressed, Venus (the black dot) slowly traced a path across the face of the sun. (Progression moves clockwise from top left.)

The successful observation elated Mason and Dixon. The Royal Society was pleased, too, especially since cloudy skies had thwarted their other authorized mission, attempted by Astronomer Royal Nevil Maskelyne on Saint Helena Island, in the South Atlantic.

Mason and Dixon's excellent results established their reputations and impressed the Penns and Frederick Calvert. The lords proprietors met with the astronomer-surveyors in 1763 and found them "Persons intirely accomplished & of good character" who would "settle & Determine" the boundary lines once and for all.

The job was immense — a surveying commission the likes of which the eighteenth-century world had never seen. With eyebrows skeptically raised, geographers, landowners, politicians, and scientists waited to see if Mason and Dixon would succeed where so many others had failed.

Chapter Seven

SURVEYORS TO THE RESCUE

BY SEPTEMBER 3, 1763, Lord Baltimore's agent (and uncle), Cecilius Calvert, had informed Maryland's governor Horatio Sharpe of the surveyors' imminent departure from London.

Mason and Dixon boarded the *Hanover Packet* and left for Pennsylvania in mid-September. After sixty-four days at sea, the two men welcomed the sight of salt-marsh grasses rippling along the fringe of Delaware Bay. Eager to be on land, they disembarked as soon as the ship dropped anchor at Marky's Hook, the first port of call for Philadelphia during colonial times, located about twenty miles south of the city. Eager to complete their journey, Mason and Dixon hired two horses—this would be the first of many horseback rides on American soil—and arrived in Philadelphia on November 15. They saw the steeples of Christ Church and the State House towering above the city's center. It was at the State House where they would formally meet with boundary-line commissioners from both provinces.

Philadelphia bustled with activity in the early 1760s. The tallest steeple belongs to Christ Church. The farthest steeple to the left is that of the State House (also shown in the left-hand inset and now called Independence Hall), where Mason and Dixon met with the commissioners.

In 1763, Philadelphia was home to about twenty thousand people — six times the number that had lived there when William Penn sailed away from the city for the final time in 1701. Wood and brick buildings lined the streets. The air was filled with a constant clamor of shopkeepers hawking their wares and harnesses jingling as carriage wheels rumbled over uneven cobblestone streets. Although these same sounds could be heard in England, the effect on the surveyors was brand-new. Philadelphia was a city of strangers. And just beyond the city's western limits were unfamiliar plants and animals. Perhaps the pair would meet native people. For the two men, America was more than a place to complete a job. It was the start of an adventure.

DOWN TO BUSINESS

Within twenty-four hours of their arrival in Philadelphia, Mason and Dixon met with Pennsylvania's boundary commissioners. They presented a letter from Thomas Penn requesting that the boundary commissioners provide instructions to the surveyors, as specified in the agreement among the surveyors, the Penns, and Lord Baltimore. An express rider galloped to Annapolis, Maryland, with a note informing Governor Sharpe of Mason and Dixon's arrival.

A flurry of activity filled the next week as Mason arranged and paid for the "landing and carriage" of their instruments to their lodgings, where he and Dixon set up and examined the zenith sector and the transit and equal altitude instrument. Inspection and testing of these crucial astronomical instruments revealed that both were in good working order.

Meanwhile, Maryland's boundary-line commissioners prepared for travel. Their arrival in Philadelphia on the last day of November heralded a week of meetings that began promptly at ten o'clock each morning. The meetings outlined Mason and Dixon's tasks, including the survey and marking of two boundary lines. One was the West Line, a 233-mile-long boundary that ran along the parallel of latitude stipulated by England's Court of Chancery as being located fifteen miles south of the southernmost point of the city of Philadelphia. (City officials had already determined that this point was the north wall of the Plumstead-Huddle house on Cedar Street, which straddled the city line.) The other line was the Tangent Line, the eastern boundary that separated Maryland from the Three Lower Counties. This line, which had defeated earlier surveyors, was Mason and Dixon's ultimate challenge. But describing Mason and Dixon's job as running two boundary lines isn't quite accurate, because surveying those lines was impossible without first completing several preliminary tasks and additional surveys. Mason and Dixon also had to prepare for the physical challenges of the terrain, as well as the looming threat of violence along the western frontier.

In the meetings, the commissioners discussed logistics such as food, tents, helpers, and wagons. They agreed they would periodically

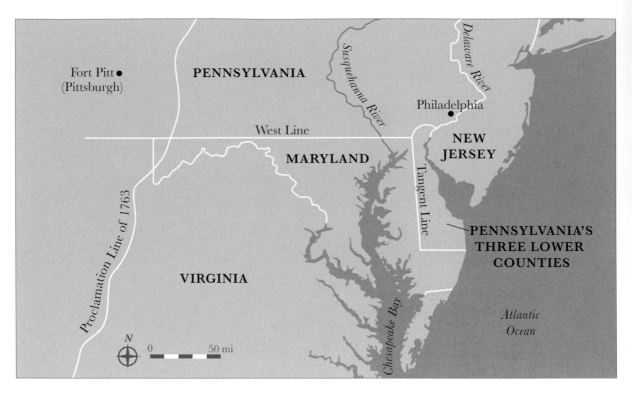

During their meeting, the commissioners and surveyors determined the order in which the boundary lines were to be surveyed. The Proclamation of 1763 forbade colonists from homesteading to the west, which was declared Indian Territory by King George III.

disburse money, supplied by the lords proprietors of both provinces, to Mason and Dixon for the payment of laborers and the purchase of supplies. Then the commissioners bickered about which boundary line should be surveyed first. Maryland commissioners insisted that the West Line—the longest line—be given top priority. They said the surveyors should survey westward until July 15 or until they reached a place called South Mountain (about ninety miles west of Philadelphia), whichever came first. They noted that Mason and Dixon could also stop if they ran into "Danger from the Incursions of the Indians." The Pennsylvania commissioners insisted that the Tangent Line be run first. They worried that "if the Business of running the Tangent Line should not be entered upon by the month of June, there would be Danger of its being unfinished till another Year, as it can be run only during the Summer Season, the land being naturally low and wet." Since Mason and Dixon's wages were paid according to the number of days they were present for the job, delays due to seasonal conditions would increase the cost of the project.

The commissioners decided that Mason and Dixon should begin with one of the preliminary tasks: determining the latitude of the southernmost point of Philadelphia. From that latitude, the surveyors could determine the line of latitude that lay fifteen miles to the south, which would be the West Line. Running the West Line without first completing this task was impossible.

An Acc.t of Cash Paid by us for the use of the Right Honbl.e Lord Baltimore, and the Hon:ble Thomas and Richard Penn Esq.rs. ————

1763

		£	s	d
Novemb: 15	Paid for the use of two Horses from Marky's Hook to Philadelphia . ———	1	10	0
22	Paid for landing, and carriage of the Instruments to our Lodgings ———	1	10	0
Decem: 15	Paid for carriage of the Instruments to y.e Observatory . .	0	15	0
	Paid for Oil and Candles ———	0	10	0
16	Paid a Smith for making Screw Drivers ———	0	05	0
	Paid for Books, Paper, Ink &c ———	0	18	6
17	Paid for Cords to secure the lids of y.e Observatory fast ———	0	03	0
	paid Men to assist in fastening the lids with the s.d Cords (it blowing a Violent storm)	0	04	6

The lords proprietors required Mason and Dixon to keep records of the monies they paid and received while running the boundary lines. This detail from a larger image of Mason's accounts lists the cash he paid out, in pounds, shillings, and pence, in the three columns on the right.

Mason and Dixon asked that their instruments be "made accessible to use in an observatory as soon as possible." Before doing so, the commissioners required Mason and Dixon to swear an oath that they would "use their best skills and knowledge and show no partiality to either Penns or Calvert." Finally, the commissioners gave Mason and Dixon a detailed set of instructions based on the decisions made during the previous week. Along with the instructions, they gave the surveyors two blank journals, with the order to document their progress:

> You are to enter fair minutes of your proceedings in two books to be by you kept for that purpose which minutes are every day to be signed by both of you and in such minutes you will take notice of the most remarkable buildings waters bridges and roads that may be near the lines which you are to run on through which the lines may pass.

Work began several days later. A carpenter hired by the commissioners built a wooden observatory on Cedar Street, near the Plumstead-Huddle house, similar to the one Mason and Dixon had used for observing the transit of Venus. Winter weather reared its head just when the surveyors were ready to begin work. Rain and snow slickened streets as winds from a "violent storm" whipped the city on December 14 and 15. Fearing that gusts would blow away the top of the observatory, Mason and Dixon wasted no time in hiring men to tie it down with cords. Even as the surveyors struggled with violent weather, news of another sort of violence reached Philadelphia.

MASSACRE!

Along Pennsylvania's western frontier, tensions between European colonists and native inhabitants had stretched to the breaking point. Territorial boundaries were definitely at stake, but cultural differences between European and native peoples also acted as a boundary that further enflamed the situation. Just months before Mason and Dixon arrived in Philadelphia, an Ottawa leader named Pontiac allied several tribes and led them in attacks against British forts and settlements in western Pennsylvania.

NATIVE PEOPLES IN THE PENNSYLVANIA AND MARYLAND PROVINCES

IN ABOUT AD 1500, five Indian nations—the Mohawk, Onondaga, Oneida, Seneca, and Cayuga—formed bonds of peace and established a league that became known as the Five Nations. Occupying areas of upstate and western New York, they called the league the Haudenosaunee, or People of the Longhouse. French explorers called them the Iroquois. Sometime around 1720, the Tuscarora Indians moved north from their homeland in North Carolina and joined the Iroquois League. Afterward, the league became known as the Six Nations. During the French and Indian War, the Iroquois allied with the British. At Grand Council assemblies, fifty sachems gathered for formal discussion and consideration of issues that concerned the welfare of the tribes. William Johnson, the king's agent for Indian affairs, regularly met with members of the Six Nations and attended Grand Council meetings when political issues arose between the colonies and the league members.

The Six Nations were not the only native peoples who lived in the area. Many others lived west of England's colonial boundaries. By the time Mason and Dixon's boundary-line survey began, decades of colonial expansion had pushed the Lenni-Lenape, whose traditional homeland lay between the Delaware and the southern Hudson Rivers, into a swatch of land across northern and western Pennsylvania and the Ohio Territory. Similarly, the Shawnee, who had lived along the Susquehanna River in eastern Pennsylvania, had been pushed back to the far western reaches of Maryland and Pennsylvania and into Ohio. Both groups had been allies of the French, and both were long-standing enemies of the Six Nations.

Other native groups had allied with English settlers. A community of about twenty Conestoga Indians lived near the town of Lancaster, on land granted to them by William Penn more than sixty years earlier. They supported themselves by growing corn and selling baskets, brooms, and other handmade goods. A colonist named Rhoda Barber later described the Conestogas as "entirely peaceable and seem'd as much afraid of the other Indians as the whites were." Almost every day, the Barber boys played with Christie, a young Conestoga boy. Christie made them bows and arrows; the brothers gave him a toy gun. The Conestogas and the settlers were neighbors and friends.

On December 13, the Paxton Boys, a gang of about fifty frontier militiamen, rode into the area. Their anger over recent Indian raids on the western and northern frontiers had long passed the boiling point. They considered all Indians their enemies, believing that even friendly Indians were secret spies. That night, revenge and retaliation filled their minds. They targeted Will Sock, a Conestoga man they suspected of conspiring with hostile Indians.

Heavy sleet and snow kept the Barber family inside their home the morning of December 14. Sudden loud knocking at their door surprised them. Opening the door, Mr. Barber found five or six men slapping snow from their coats. They said they were cold and asked to warm themselves at the Barbers' hearth. Upholding the frontier code of hospitality to travelers, Mr. Barber invited them in and offered them hot refreshments. While the men talked, the Barber boys snuck outside to look at the men's horses. Blood-covered tomahawks dangled from the saddles. Even more frightening, Christie's toy gun hung among them. As soon as the men left, the boys told their father what they'd seen. Even as Mr. Barber was deciding what to do, a neighbor arrived with shocking news: men had attacked the Conestogas and set their homes afire.

Mr. Barber and his friends hurried to the Conestogas' land. Among the still-smoldering ruins, they found the bodies of six of their Indian neighbors—three men, two women, and a boy. All had been horribly murdered. Christie was missing.

A MOST MIRACULOUS INSTRUMENT

News of the massacre quickly spread to Philadelphia. Charles Mason later recorded information about the massacre in his journal, so there is little doubt that the surveyors discussed the disturbing events while the story was breaking news. Despite unsettled minds, their commissioned job required them to turn their attention to the work of determining the latitude of the southernmost point of Philadelphia.

Mason and Dixon's first order of business was setting up their telescope in their newly constructed observatory. They would be using a vertically mounted telescope called a zenith sector, made by English astronomer John Bird. Mason would be using it to measure an angle called the zenith distance. A zenith distance is the angle created between a star's position on the celestial sphere, an observer standing on Earth, and the zenith, the point on the celestial sphere directly above the observer. Once Mason knew a star's zenith distance, as measured with the sector, and the star's declination (the celestial equivalent of latitude), which he could find in the Royal Society's star table, he could mathematically calculate the latitude of the spot where the zenith sector was located.

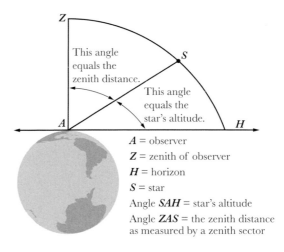

A = observer
Z = zenith of observer
H = horizon
S = star
Angle **SAH** = star's altitude
Angle **ZAS** = the zenith distance as measured by a zenith sector

In order to compute his latitude, Charles Mason first used a special telescope called a zenith sector to measure the angle between his zenith and a chosen star.

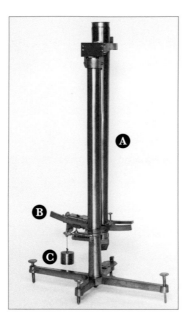

This is a zenith sector, similar to the one Mason used. (A) is the telescope; (B) is the sector, used for measuring the zenith distance; and (C) is the plumb bob, used to ensure that the instrument was vertical.

Using the zenith sector was a multistep process. First, Mason fastened the sector's stand to a stable base and adjusted it until it was absolutely level. Next, he mounted the telescope vertically in the stand. The telescope, which pointed straight up, could pivot, so Mason could adjust its position during his observations. A slightly curved scale called a sector was attached to the instrument's base. The sector was a small segment of an arc taken from a circle that had a six-foot radius. The sector was inscribed with increments of degrees. A plumb bob was suspended from the sector so that Mason could make sure the instrument was perfectly vertical.

Because the eyepiece of the telescope was near the ground, Mason had to lie flat on his back to use it. When peering through the eyepiece, he saw two very fine wires—one horizontal and one vertical—that crossed each other, perpendicularly, exactly in the center of the telescope's view. Since Mason used the telescope at night, Dixon (or another helper) would illuminate the wires by holding a candle alongside a hole in the side of the eyepiece.

Brought the Instrument in to the Meridian by making several Stars pass along the Horizontal wire in the middle of the Telescope

The method pursu'd in doing of this is as follows.

Let HO the Horizontal, and NS the Vertical wires, then, we bring a Northern star (one as for N. of ƴ Zenith as ƴ limits of ƴ arch) to the Horizontal wire at a, and it will describe the arch of a circle as abc, (the Telescope inverting).

If ap be apparently equal to pc, it is truly in the Meridian, if not equal, we proceed by Trial, till they are equal; which may be done with 4 or 5 Stars to great exactness, as we find by comparing the time of the stars passing the wire NS, with the time they Transit the Meridian as found by Equal Altitudes. ——

17 Cloudy

18 Cloudy

*mag:	Stars Names	✳ R.	nearest point on ƴ Sector	Revo: & Sec on ƴ Microm:	Difference	App: Zen: Dist: Plane of ƴ Sector faceing th. East.
		h '	° '	A ''	B ''	''
19	δ Persei		7.5 — {	10.20 / 11.9½	0.41,5	7.4.18,5	x
	Capella	4.59	5.50 — {	2.39½ / 5.46	3.6,5	5.47.17,5	x
	κ Urs: Majo:		8.5 + {	5.26½ / 2.33+	2.45,2	8.7.29,2	
20	α Lyræ		1.20 + {	9.29½ / 11.47	2.17,5	1.22.1,5	x
	γ Androm:		1.15 — {	7.32 / 7.41	0.9,0	1.14.51,0	
	β Persei		0.5 + {	10.16½ / 9.43½	0.25,0	0.5.25,0	
	δ Persei		7.5 — {	8.43 / 9.34½	0.43,5	7.4.16,5	
	Capella		5.50 — {	6.24½ / 9.24½	3.0,0	5.47.24,0	
	β Aurigæ		4.55 + {	5.40½ / 3.11	2.29,5	4.57.13,5	N.

A page from Mason's daily journal. The circular diagram at the top shows the crossed wires he saw when peering through the telescope of the zenith sector. Arc *abc*, which dips below the horizontal wire, shows the path of a star as time passes. The names and positions of the stars Mason observed are recorded on the bottom half of the page. Mason used the stars' Greek and Latin names.

HOW LONG IS A DAY?

*I*N RELATION TO THE SUN, *Earth completes one revolution on its axis (360 degrees) every twenty-four hours. Astronomers call this one solar day. Our clocks are designed to operate relative to the solar day. But relative to a star's fixed position, Earth completes its 360-degree revolution in twenty-three hours and fifty-six minutes, slightly faster than a solar day. Astronomers call the rotation with respect to the stars a sidereal day. Earth is divided into twenty-four sidereal hours, the same as right ascension. In fact, the local sidereal time is always equal to the right ascension of any star that lies on the observer's meridian. (Sidereal time and the time on a clock do not always match. For that reason, Mason and Dixon recorded both sidereal time and the time measured by a pendulum clock.)*

A star's position in the celestial sphere is fixed. Right ascension and declination, like longitude and latitude on Earth's surface, pinpoint the star's location. But a sidereal day's shorter length affects the clock time of when we first see a star at night. As measured by a clock, a star rises almost four minutes earlier each night. For example, on June 1, a particular star first appears above the horizon at 10:00 p.m. On June 2, it rises at 9:56 p.m., when one full rotation of Earth, relative to that star, has been completed. On June 3, the star rises at 9:52 p.m. After a month, the star's first appearance above the horizon is nearly two hours earlier (120 minutes divided by 60 minutes equals 2 hours) than when it first rose on June 1.

If we kept clocks relative to sidereal time, noon would gradually shift four minutes a day until lunchtime would be in the middle of the night. The four-minute discrepancy between solar time and star time makes a big difference when it is part of an equation being used to plot one's location on Earth. For that reason, Mason and Dixon meticulously tested the accuracy of their pendulum clock or a pocket watch by noting whether the clocks were gaining or losing time when compared with sidereal time.

No Accuracy without Alignment

Mason pointed the sector's telescope at the sky through an opening in the observatory's roof. His first task was to align the zenith sector in the meridian, the north-south celestial line directly above him. The accuracy of all of his observations depended on getting this alignment exactly right. To align the sector, he watched four or five stars, one after another, pass across the wires in his view. Because of Earth's rotation, during the course of a night, each star would appear to travel across the sky in an arc-shaped path parallel to the celestial equator. As the star moved across the telescope's view, the arc of its path carried it across the horizontal wire twice—once on each side of the vertical wire. Dixon recorded the exact times when each star crossed the two wires. When a star crossed the vertical wire, the highest point of the arc, the star was on the meridian. Using the positions of the stars and the times when they were on the meridian, Mason could adjust the position of the zenith sector so that it, too, was in the meridian.

Mason double-checked the sector's results by dividing by two the time that lapsed between the first and second times a star crossed the horizontal wire. On subsequent nights, if the sector was correct, the clock or watch would confirm that a star crossed the vertical wire halfway between the two points in time. Mason repeated this comparison many times during the course of the boundary-line survey.

With the zenith sector accurately aligned with the meridian and pointing vertically at the opening in the roof, Mason and Dixon began collecting the information necessary to determine the latitude of Philadelphia's southernmost point. They had chosen ten specific stars to observe and track. Weather permitting, even on Christmas night, they looked at and recorded information about five or six of those ten. Mason slightly tilted the telescope until he centered a star in the cross wires. Then he measured the star's zenith distance with the micrometer,

1763	Stars Name	R's	nearest point on ye Sector	Revolutions & Seconds on ye Microm:	Diff:	Apt. Zen. dist Plane of ye Sector West	☿.' N° or S°
Dec:							
30							

Equal Altitude
of Capella:

Time per Watch.
R. "	R. "
3·50·32	5·55·41
51·35	56·58
52·54	58·11

} Hence Capella pass'd the Merid:ⁿ ⅌ Transit

Instrument at 4ʰ·54·18 and it was Obs:ᵈ to pass the Vertical wire in the Sector at 4ʰ·54·7".

1763	Stars Name	R's	nearest point on ye Sector	Revolutions & Seconds	Diff:	Apt. Zen. dist	☿
			o · '	R · "		o · ' · "	
31	α Lyræ	1·20+	{ 11·45 / 9·28 }	R " / 2·17		1·22·1,0	
	γ Androm:	1·15−	{ 6·3 / 6·18½ }	0·6,5		1·14·53,5	
1764							
January							
☉ 1	γ Androm:	1·15−	{ 6·19,7 / 6·13,3 }	0·6,4		1·14·53,6	
	β Persei	0·5+	{ 7·22 / 8·1½ }	0·31,5		0·5·31,5	
	Capella	5·50−	{ 11·28 / 8·35 }	2·45,0		5·47·31,0	
	β Aurigæ	4·55+	{ 8·26+ / 11·13 }	2·38,7		4·57·22,7	
	Castor	7·35−	{ 11·4 / 13·3 }	1·51,0		7·33·17,0	
	x Urs: Majo:	8·5+	{ 12·41 / 15·45− }	3·3,7		8·7·39,7	
2	γ Androm:	1·15−	{ 11·33½ / 11·27 }	0·6,5		1·14·53,5	
	β Persei	0·5+	{ 10·27½ / 11·5½ }	0·30,0		0·5·30,0	
	α Persei	9·5−	{ 13·47 / 12·20 }	1·27,0		9·3·41,0	
	δ Persei	7·5−	{ 13·22+ / 12·35 }	0·39,3		7·4·20,7	
	Capella	5·50−	{ 13·5 / 10·11½ }	2·45,5		5·47·30,5	

√

This page from Mason's journal records the stars he observed from December 30, 1763, through January 2, 1764, and their positions in the sky.

a very precise measuring device attached to the telescope. No other scientific instrument of the period surpassed the accuracy of John Bird's zenith sector. It could accurately measure the angle of the zenith distance to within a fraction of seconds of a degree of arc. From December 19, 1763, to January 4, 1764, the two surveyors made many observations. They recorded the zenith distances of select stars. They noted right ascensions. They wrote down the sidereal times of the selected stars and compared them with times noted on the observatory's clock. They consulted the star tables for declination. Mason and Dixon were delighted with the sector's precision and were confident they would soon know the latitude of the southernmost point of Philadelphia.

MORE BAD NEWS

Unfortunately, the good news of the sector's success was tempered by upsetting news as more information concerning the Conestoga Indians filtered into Philadelphia. Young Christie, awakened by gunshots and screams, had escaped from his house. He had run to the home of Captain Thomas McKee and told him what had happened—including the fact that thirteen Conestogas had been away from home at the time. Christie didn't know what had happened to those still at home.

According to rumors, the Paxton Boys still intended to kill Will Sock, who was not among the dead. Fearing for the remaining Conestogas' safety, local magistrate Edward Shippen placed them into protective custody. By December 17, fourteen Conestogas—four men, three women, three little girls, and four young boys, including Christie—sheltered inside Lancaster's new brick workhouse, guarded by the sheriff. Express riders galloped messages between township and provincial authorities. Officials requested that anyone with information about the perpetrators of the crime step forward. John Penn, the governor of Pennsylvania and

After the Paxton Boys' December 27 massacre of the Conestogas in Lancaster, their mob grew. Nearly 250 men, angered by Indian attacks on the colonial frontier, reached the outskirts of Philadelphia. Benjamin Franklin and other community leaders persuaded them not to storm the city.

a grandson of William Penn, issued a proclamation for the capture of the men who had "inhumanly killed six of the Indians."

Meanwhile, the Paxton Boys readied themselves for another attack. At midafternoon on December 27, between eighty and one hundred men carrying "Muskets, Tomahawks, & Scalping knives" rode into Lancaster. They dismounted and walked to the workhouse. Threatened by the armed mob, Sheriff John Hay and the coroner, Matthias Slough, stepped aside. The Paxton Boys broke in the workhouse door and, in a manner even more brutal than the first attack, massacred the unarmed Conestogas inside. No one escaped. After less than twelve minutes, the Paxton Boys left the workhouse, mounted their horses, and rode out of town. None of them was ever caught.

The news of the Lancaster murders further horrified Mason and Dixon. But they still needed to continue their work. By the end of the first week of January 1764, the surveyors had finally finished stargazing. Mason completed his calculations. (Without calculators or computers, several days of mathematical computation always followed long periods of observing the stars.) After two days, he informed the commissioners that the latitude of the southernmost point of Philadelphia was 39 degrees 56 minutes 29.1 seconds north (39°56'29.1" N).

TO HARLAN'S HOUSE

With one preliminary task accomplished, the surveyors moved on to the second: surveying to a point fifteen miles south of their current location—which would be the latitude for the West Line, the long boundary line that ran east to west between the provinces. However, traveling directly south fifteen miles and then turning west would have required surveying across the wide Delaware River twice. Mason and Dixon avoided the unnecessary inconvenience by first riding thirty miles west of the southernmost point of Philadelphia to a location where they could survey southward far from the course of the Delaware River.

Richard Peters, one of Pennsylvania's boundary commissioners, had assisted the survey crew in running a temporary boundary line in 1739. Peters knew that wilderness travel was arduous. Before Mason and Dixon left town, he sent them a friendly letter that began, "Gentleman: I hope you have pleased yourselves with good horses and an agreeable companion." Their companion may have been Joel Baily, a clockmaker and gunsmith, who lived three miles from the surveyors' destination. An experienced surveyor, Baily was also interested in astronomy. He accompanied them to John Harlan's home, at the fork of Brandywine Creek. Harlan, a Quaker, agreed to board the surveyors and also told them they could erect their wooden observatory in his garden. In the years that followed, Harlan's sturdy stone house would become Mason and Dixon's American home. They would come to know Harlan's wife, Sarah, and their five children as if they were family.

John Harlan's stone house, at the fork of Brandywine Creek, became Mason and Dixon's home away from home while they were in America.

For now, Mason and Dixon returned to Philadelphia and prepared to move west. Two carpenters dismantled the observatory and "put [it] with the rest of our Instruments into the wagons." The surveyors feared that a bone-rattling two-day wagon ride would damage the zenith sector, so rather than loading it with the other instruments, it was wrapped, boxed, and then "carried on the Springs (with Feather bed under it) of a single Horse chair [carriage]." Both carpenters accompanied the surveyors back to Harlan's house.

Eager to begin, Mason and Dixon set up the zenith sector inside a tent in the garden. They used the stars Capella and Beta Aurigae to confirm their location. The zenith sector's measurements pleased Mason: "Finding we were very near the Parallel [of latitude] of the southernmost point of Philadelphia, we ordered Carpenters to Erect the Observatory."

The surveyors sent regular dispatches to the boundary commissioners to report their progress. At the end of January, Mason wrote to Commissioner Peters,

> I've here the pleasure to acquaint you that all our Instruments came here without receiving the least damage. By the few observations we have made, our situation is not far from the Parallel requir'd. As soon as we have settled the south end of the 15 miles, we shall not fail to acquaint you of it. A great number of Labourers will then be wanted.

Occasionally, Mason interjected a personal request. Thinking of letters from his family that might arrive in Philadelphia during his absence, he noted to Peters:

> When I left Philadelphia I desired the Post Master to deliver my Letters (if any should come from England) to you, a freedom I humbly beg you will pardon, and be pleas'd to keep them 'till opportunity serve to send them to hand and the favour will always be acknowledg'd.

During January and February, Mason and Dixon came to know John Harlan's yard well. But working in the garden was no picnic. They slogged through slush after mid-January snows. They shivered until the observatory's broken stove was mended. And even afterward, being in the observatory was still colder than sitting by the large fireplace in the Harlans' home. At the end of a long night's work, they were glad to climb the steep stairs up to their beds in the warm house.

By the end of February, Mason and Dixon had determined that the latitude of the observatory in Harlan's garden was 39°56'18.9" north. This was 10.5 seconds of latitude farther south than the southernmost point of Philadelphia. Mason noted the difference in his journal. He would account for this difference mathematically later, when he and Dixon were fifteen miles farther south and determining the actual latitude of the West Line. Finally, with the latitude of Harlan's garden established, they began their second preliminary task: measuring to the parallel of latitude that was fifteen miles south.

Nearly two weeks of gray skies, snow, and rain delayed them, leaving everyone as gloomy and cold as the weather. One evening, during a short break in the "flying clouds," Mason observed the polestar, also known as the North Star or Polaris, just as it crossed the meridian directly above him. Mason realized that physically marking the meridian's location on the ground would be a daytime anchor for Dixon's instrument and make his surveying work easier. To mark the meridian's location, the surveyors turned a large, oblong rock on end and settled it in the soil—a digging job that was likely assigned to the considerably younger backs of the Harlans' oldest sons, Phinehas and Jesse.

The Stargazer's Stone, placed in the Harlans' yard, anchored Mason and Dixon to the meridian.

But cloudy skies during his observation of the polestar left Mason questioning the accuracy of the rock's placement. A week later, under clear skies, Mason observed the polestar again and had his crew reposition the rock to mark the meridian more accurately. Dixon often used the rock as a benchmark when surveying and measuring distances from the observatory. It wasn't long before the Harlans and their neighbors started calling the large rock the Stargazer's Stone.

On Sunday, March 17, the night sky offered a special treat: a lunar eclipse. Though Mason had seen many eclipses, the spectacular event impressed him: "The edge of the Sun's Shadow on the Moons disk was the best defined I ever saw." Afterward, clear skies and clear weather allowed the survey party to begin its fifteen-mile trek south.

Chapter  Eight

TACKLING THE
IMPOSSIBLE

CHARLES MASON, with his expertise in astronomy and mathematics, directed the duo's work during the early weeks of the boundary-line mission. Dixon's expertise as a surveyor took center stage as the focus shifted from the stars to the ground. But before Dixon could begin his work, he needed a vista—a clear line of sight—along the meridian he planned to follow south. Within forty-eight hours of the lunar eclipse, four axmen, wood chips flying, steadily cut a "visto in the Meridian Southward."

Surveying across the land required using different instruments from those Mason had used so far. The zenith sector, perfect for measuring angles on the celestial sphere, couldn't sight or measure land distances. Instead, Dixon used a circumferentor, an instrument that looks like a large compass with built-in leveling bubbles and two upright bars used to sight distant objects. A circumferentor indicates direction (north, south, east, and west) and can measure horizontal angles that are necessary for accurate land surveys. The land survey also required the addition of a few new crew members, all with previous surveying experience.

Dixon used this circumferentor to keep the chain crew on course as they surveyed south from Harlan's garden. The instrument in the middle is a compass, and the two liquid-filled tubes are levels.

In Harlan's garden, outside the observatory, Dixon aligned his circumferentor with the meridian. A crewman stood several hundred feet away, holding a wooden stake. Dixon peered through the instrument's sighting slits (one on each upright bar) and signaled the crewman to move right or left until the stake was aligned with the instrument's sights. Aligning the crewman with the two sights ensured a straight line. After setting the stake in place, it was time to haul out the chain—a two-man job.

CHAINS, LINKS, AND LEVELS

Under Dixon's direction, two chain carriers measured a distance from the circumferentor with a surveyor's tool called a Gunter's chain. This sixty-six-foot-long metal chain consists of one hundred links, each of which is 7.92 inches long. A link of a Gunter's chain is formed from a straight metal bar. Each end of the bar is bent to form a small circle. Small measured metal circles connect the links. Eighty chains equal one mile (5,280 feet). One chain carrier firmly anchored the end of the chain at the starting point outside the observatory. The other chain carrier unfolded the chain as he walked toward the distant wooden stake. When the chain was completely extended, he stopped walking and stretched the chain taut. On the ground, he marked the spot beneath the end of the chain with an iron pin. This completed one chain.

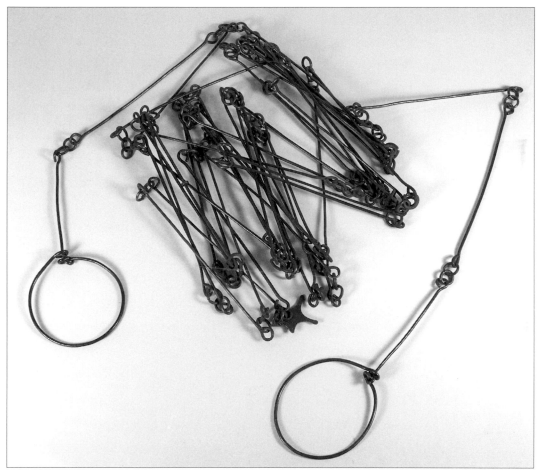

A Gunter's chain was the chain bearers' constant companion. From time to time, the circles connecting the links became stretched out and had to be reshaped to keep the length of the chain accurate.

Keeping a tally, Dixon and the chain carriers repeated these steps until they reached the distant wooden stake or a land feature that created an obstacle, such as a creek. At 9 chains and 61 links (634 feet 3.12 inches) from Harlan's garden, the crew reached the sloped bank of Brandywine Creek. Surveying up or down a slope with a chain is difficult, if not impossible. Plus, measuring directly along the ground up and down short, steep slopes would have considerably shortened how far south the fifteen-mile line extended, something the Pennsylvania commissioners vociferously opposed. Dixon's men replaced the Gunter's chain with a wooden rod called a level that was twenty-two feet long.

To measure the distance from the top of the creek bank to the water's edge as a straight rather than sloped line, two chain carriers held a level, one man at each end, so that neither end was higher or lower than the other. Two more crewmen stepped into place, holding one end of a second level directly beneath the front end of the first level. As the crewmen repeated this process, Dixon and his circumferentor kept them on course by aligning the men with a stake placed on the meridian across the creek. It took the crew four levels, or steps, to reach the edge of Brandywine Creek closest to Harlan's house.

Brandywine Creek loops around near the Harlan house. Before Dixon's men had surveyed a mile, Mason noted that they'd splashed across the creek three times. That meant the crewmen had to work in sopping-wet leather shoes or boots and wet wool pants, which may not have dried out during the day, due to chilly air temperatures. Most colonists owned few changes of clothes and only one pair of shoes; changing outfits frequently was not an option. So the waders squelched when they walked, and their legs itched as wet wool chafed their skin. A long hike in these conditions was uncomfortable, as was using the difficult-to-maneuver twenty-two-foot-long levels. After crossing Brandywine Creek once, the crew switched to less cumbersome levels that were only sixteen and a half feet long. As they proceeded south, the men became an efficient and precise survey team.

Periodically, Mason observed the stars to confirm that the line was still true to the meridian of Harlan's garden (or to determine how the line needed to be shifted if it had veered off course). On April 5, he noted with satisfaction that he had "Proved the Meridian and found it very exact." In addition to checking their course, Mason and Dixon also had to check their Gunter's chain. Repeatedly pulling the chain taut could cause the wire circles at the end of each link to stretch slightly, making the chain inaccurate. Mason and Dixon measured the links' length against a three-foot-long brass rod. They reshaped any links that had lengthened. On April 5, Mason "Found the chain a little too long. Corrected it." When he measured the chain again on April 9 and 12, it was exact. The Penns and Lord Baltimore had hired Mason and Dixon as the best men for the job, and the best is what they got.

By April 12, the crew had traveled over fourteen miles. Now was the time to account for the fact that their starting point, at the observatory in Harlan's garden, was *already* 10.5 seconds south of Philadelphia's southernmost point. That distance had to be included in the overall length of their fifteen-mile-long line south. Mathematically, Mason converted the seconds into yards. He found that 10.5 seconds of a degree of latitude was equal to 357 yards. This distance is more than three and a half times the length of a football field. While that may not seem like much, if the line were placed that much too far south and extended west over the 233-mile-long distance, the acreage added to Pennsylvania's area would add up. In fact, if the acreage involved were reconfigured as a chunk of land rather than a long, thin strip, it would occupy an area the size of Disney World or the city of San Francisco. The Maryland commissioners would never have ceded that much land to Pennsylvania.

SEASONAL CHANGES

*I*T TAKES THE EARTH *one year to orbit the sun. Because Earth's axis is tilted, during half of the year, one hemisphere receives more sunlight than the other, creating the summer season. Earth's tilt also affects the seasonal visibility of certain stars. For example, in December 1763, when Mason and Dixon first began observations in Philadelphia, Capella, one of the brightest stars in the sky, quickly caught their eyes. In the Northern Hemisphere, Capella is a star of the fall and winter sky and would not be visible in July.*

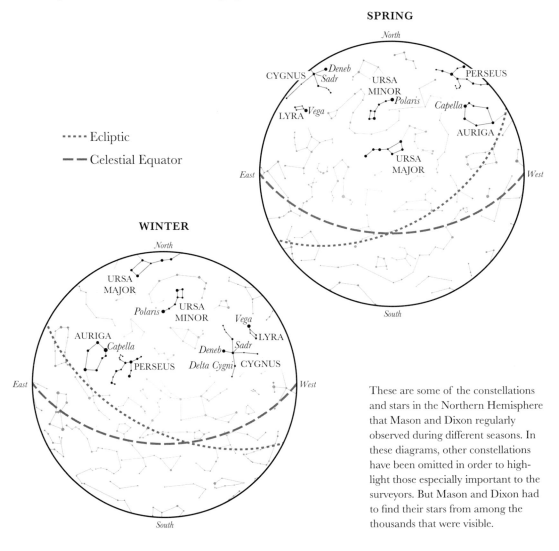

These are some of the constellations and stars in the Northern Hemisphere that Mason and Dixon regularly observed during different seasons. In these diagrams, other constellations have been omitted in order to highlight those especially important to the surveyors. But Mason and Dixon had to find their stars from among the thousands that were visible.

During the summer, Earth's tilt and orbital position placed Capella below Mason's horizon. Seasonally, Mason and Dixon adjusted which stars they observed according to their visibility. The North Star, also called Polaris, is almost straight north of Earth's axis. It is unaffected by the annual orbit and is visible in the Northern Hemisphere year round, as are the stars that closely surround it.

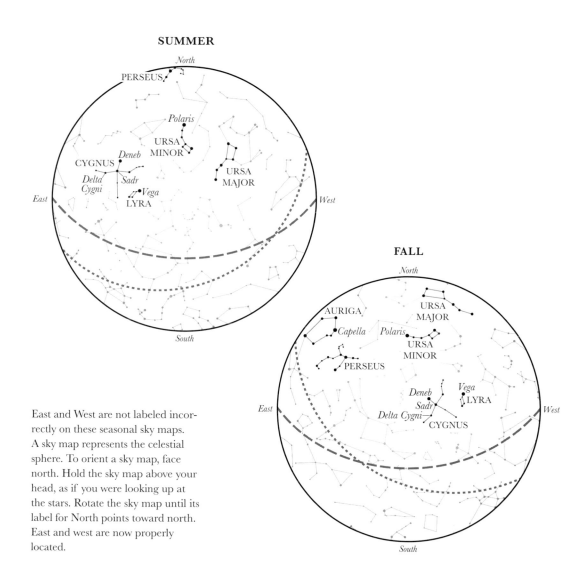

East and West are not labeled incorrectly on these seasonal sky maps. A sky map represents the celestial sphere. To orient a sky map, face north. Hold the sky map above your head, as if you were looking up at the stars. Rotate the sky map until its label for North points toward north. East and west are now properly located.

Mason then converted 357 yards to chains, arriving at the figure 16.23 chains. Dixon added this to the number of chains he and the chain bearers had already measured southward from Harlan's garden. Together, the figures added up to 15 miles, 2 chains, and 93 links. The crew's journey south was complete. The end of the fifteen-mile line was on squishy, damp land owned by a man named Alexander Bryan.

During the next week, the crew returned to Harlan's farm, dismantled the observatory, and packed the instruments into four wagons—Mason employing "five Laborers in carrying one of the instruments," most likely the zenith sector. Then they returned to the end of the fifteen-mile line,

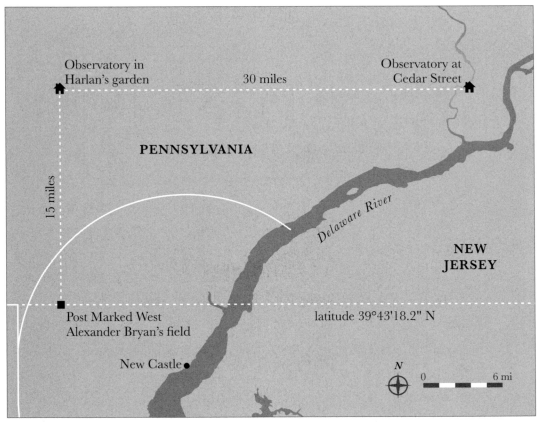

After their trip west from Philadelphia, Mason and Dixon prepared themselves for another trek, this time directly south, in their quest for the latitude of the West Line.

where five men, hammering in the rain, reconstructed the observatory. Meanwhile, Mason and Dixon rode to Philadelphia, where they met with the commissioners to report their progress and receive further instructions.

By June 9, the surveyors had determined that the latitude of the southern end of the fifteen-mile line was 39 degrees 43 minutes 18.2 seconds north (39°43'18.2" N). This latitude would be the very long east-west boundary line, called the West Line, between Maryland and Pennsylvania. They marked the spot with a wooden post set several feet deep in the ground and called the marker the Post Marked West. They carved the word WEST into the side facing west. Then, following the commissioners' instructions, the surveyors turned their attention to the Tangent Line, determined to succeed where so many colonial surveyors had failed.

The Tangent Line

The commissioners expected Mason and Dixon to begin work on the Tangent Line, Maryland's eighty-mile-long eastern border, by June 15, 1764. With that date fast approaching, Mason and Dixon began assembling a larger crew and plenty of provisions. Knowing that John Vause's apothecary shop, on the corner of Market and Third Streets in Philadelphia, supplied medicine chests for ship captains, the army, and the navy, Mason ordered a large box stocked with medicines and remedies for treating cuts, fevers, snakebites, and stomach ailments— anything likely to plague a sick or injured crewman on the trail.

Running a large crew was a full-time job. On the recommendation of the commissioners, Mason and Dixon hired twenty-six-year-old Moses McClean as their steward, a position he had held during the previous Tangent Line survey. (His older brother Archibald had been a surveyor on the 1760 crew.) In this capacity, McClean purchased food, tents, and horses. He handled monies sent by the commissioners, took care of payroll logistics, hired crewmen as needed, and oversaw equipment maintenance, arranging for repairs when necessary. In short, McClean was Mason and Dixon's go-to man. Without him, they could not have focused their full attention on the survey.

Surveying the Tangent Line took Mason and Dixon on their first long American journey. A distance of eighty miles separated the two ends of the line—the southern end, at a spot called the Middle Point, and the northern end, at the tangent point. The surveyors had to travel nearly the whole length of the peninsula shared by Maryland and Pennsylvania before they could start their new task. Under McClean's supervision, the crew struck camp in Mr. Bryan's field and packed their gear into the wagons. The surveyors stored their astronomical instruments at a nearby home, a practice that became routine. The team then made its way to New Castle, where Mason and Dixon found comfortable lodgings at an inn, a welcome change from camp life. After rehiring old hands from the Brandywine, McClean and the crew departed for the Middle Point, where work on the Tangent Line would begin.

By the time everyone reached the bank of the Nanticoke River, the crew had swelled to thirty-nine men and the camp bustled with activity. While the axmen honed their blades, tent keepers pounded tent pegs into the ground. Cooks lit fires and prepared the evening meal. Wagoners unhitched their teams and tethered the horses. Moses McClean didn't want any runaway horses. Two of the horses used during the 1760 Tangent Line survey had strayed from camp, and he'd had to offer a reward for them in the *Pennsylvania Gazette*. That same issue contained notices about three more lost horses, three found horses, and two stolen horses. Horses were a necessity in colonial America. So McClean and his wagon drivers kept a sharp eye on their animals, cared for them well, and tethered them securely.

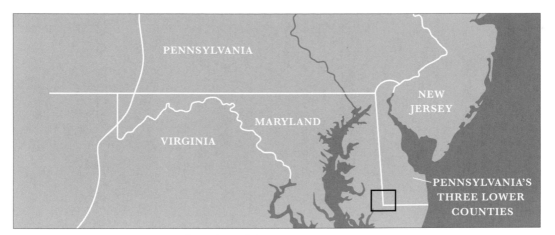

The black rectangle inset is the area of the Middle Point.

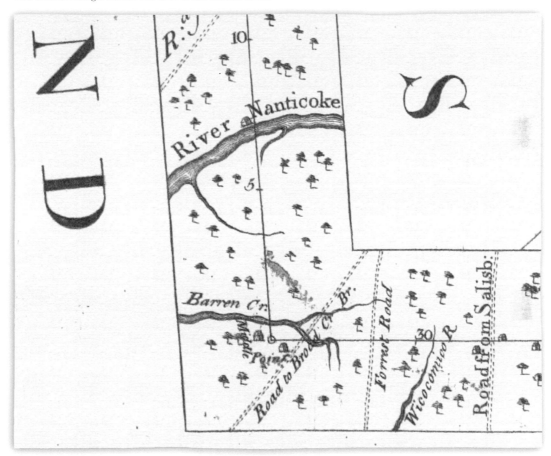

Jeremiah Dixon's final map of the boundary line included details such as the Nanticoke River, which they crossed north of the Middle Point.

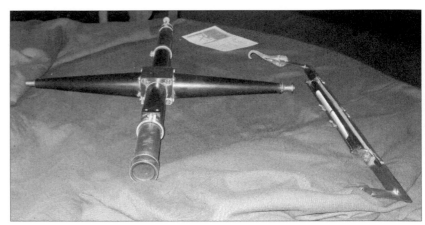

Left: A transit and equal altitude instrument mounted on a tripod. Above: The telescope and level of Dixon's transit. The transit on the tripod is missing a level. Dixon always suspended a level from his telescope to ensure that the transit was level at all times, which was crucial for accurate measurements. He probably used a tripod but may also have supported the transit on a tree stump.

FOLLOWING THE BEAR'S TAIL

A boundary-line survey must be accurate. No matter how hard the 1760–1763 survey team had tried, surveying the Tangent Line had defeated them; the lines they surveyed had always missed the tangent point along the arc of the circle drawn around New Castle. Rather than attempting an eighty-mile-long survey line aimed at the tangent point (as the earlier survey crews had), Mason just decided to run an eighty-mile-long straight line, knowing that it would end a bit west of the tangent point. Mason planned to then shift their straight line, first mathematically and then, with Dixon's surveying expertise, physically, until it touched the tangent point. But for Mason's plan to work, he needed a guiding star to keep Dixon and the chain carriers on an absolutely straight path for eighty miles.

ACCURATE TO THE MINUTE

*A*N ACCURATE WATCH *was essential to the success of Mason and Dixon's survey. Dixon tested the accuracy of their watch with the transit and equal altitude instrument. First he placed the instrument on the Middle Point. A crewman set a new wooden post half a mile due north of the Middle Point, close to the first wooden marking post set by the 1760 Tangent Line crew. Since it was dark outside, the crewman placed a lit candle atop the post so Dixon could sight the new wooden post with the instrument's telescope. Despite Dixon's distance from the candle, he easily saw the flame because no other outside lighting existed to overwhelm it.*

Looking into the telescope of the transit and equal altitude instrument, Dixon saw one horizontal cross wire and three vertical cross wires. The vertical wires were perpendicular to the horizontal wire. The middle vertical wire crossed the horizontal wire at the center of the viewing lens. When the candle flame was centered, Dixon tightened screws on the telescope that prevented it from shifting to the left or right. The transit and equal altitude instrument was now aligned with the meridian (the direction true north) for that location. Then he tilted the telescope skyward on the instrument's vertical axis and tightened it in place so it couldn't shift up or down. Finally, he looked through the telescope and waited for a specific star to transit, or cross, the horizontal wire in the viewing lens. Mason recorded the hour, minute, and second when it did. As Dixon kept watch, Mason also recorded the exact hour, minute, and second when that same star transited each of the vertical wires.

During the course of a night, Earth's rotation causes the stars to appear as though they are traveling westward across the sky in an arc-shaped path. Dixon monitored the star's path until it transited the horizontal wire a second time, this time on the opposite side of the three vertical wires. Mason recorded that time, too. By dividing the time that elapsed between the star's first and second crossings of the horizontal wire in half, Mason and Dixon knew the exact time when the star reached its zenith, or highest point in the sky, according to their watch. At that point, the star crossed the meridian — the line that encircles the celestial sphere in a north-south direction. This precise time was another piece of information Mason and Dixon factored into their calculations. If the watch gained or lost time when compared to established times published in the star tables provided by the Royal Society, Mason needed to compensate mathematically for the difference. Satisfied that their watch was accurate, they began to implement Mason's creative plan for running the Tangent Line.

The star Mason chose is named Delta Ursae Minoris, located in the constellation Ursa Minor, the Little Bear. Delta Ursae Minoris is the second star in the bear's tail. Mason didn't note why he chose this star, but it is close to the North Star and is directionally north, which was generally the direction they were heading. And unlike the North Star, whose position doesn't shift measurably, Delta Ursae Minoris appears to move in an arc that Dixon could easily observe with the transit and equal altitude instrument. These observations would provide Mason with the data he needed for his calculations that would enable them to remain steadfastly on a straight course.

As he had done during the watch test, a crewman placed a lighted candle atop the recently set wooden post half a mile north of the Middle Point. Dixon centered the flame in the viewing lens of the transit and equal altitude's telescope and tightened the scope to prevent it from shifting to the left or right.

As he had done before, Dixon tipped the telescope skyward and fixed it in place. Then he and Mason waited for Delta Ursae Minoris to appear. Slowly, as the minutes ticked by, the small star moved into view and approached the horizontal cross wire. Mason noted the exact hour, minute, and second when it first touched the horizontal cross wire, as well as the second time it did so. In the daytime, with the transit's alignment still firmly fixed in place, Dixon lowered the telescope and directed a chain carrier, who stood at a point some distance away, to move his position until he was precisely aligned with Dixon's transit. Then Dixon instructed the other chain carriers to measure the distance to that man. They did so using the same procedure they had used in 1764 when surveying to the point fifteen miles south from the observatory in John Harlan's garden. Chain after chain, the crew surveyed a straight line northwestward, marking each new mile with a wooden post. Meanwhile, Mason consulted the sidereal times in the Royal Society's

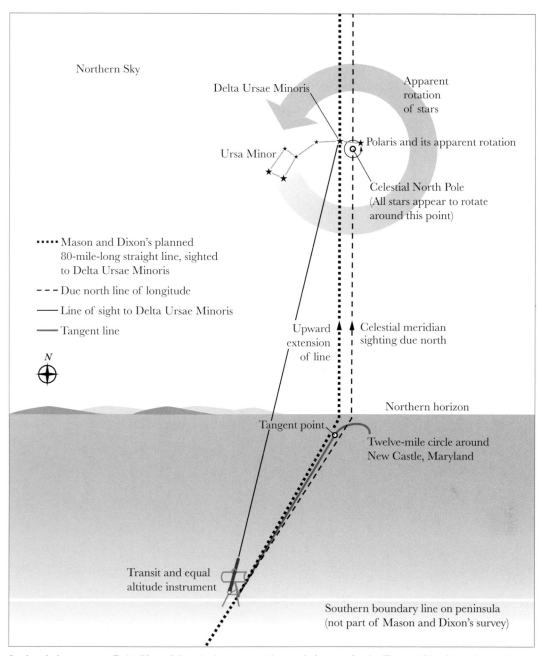

Northern Sky

Delta Ursae Minoris

Apparent rotation of stars

Ursa Minor

★ Polaris and its apparent rotation

Celestial North Pole
(All stars appear to rotate around this point)

•••• Mason and Dixon's planned 80-mile-long straight line, sighted to Delta Ursae Minoris

- - - Due north line of longitude

—— Line of sight to Delta Ursae Minoris

—— Tangent line

N

Upward extension of line

Celestial meridian sighting due north

Northern horizon

Tangent point

Twelve-mile circle around New Castle, Maryland

Transit and equal altitude instrument

Southern boundary line on peninsula
(not part of Mason and Dixon's survey)

Setting their course on Delta Ursae Minoris, the surveyors began their quest for the Tangent Line by setting up the transit and equal altitude instrument at the Middle Point. Stargazing at night and measuring with a Gunter's chain during the day, the surveyors moved in a slightly northwestern direction until they'd traveled more than eighty miles.

star tables and compared them to the times he and Dixon noted. Mason needed this information for mathematical computations that would help him precisely establish the Tangent Line at a later date. For the next two months, Dixon's task was to keep the transit and equal altitude instrument precisely aligned with the course set by Delta Ursae Minoris. At every fifth milepost, the chain carriers measured the offset, or distance, between the new posts they were setting along their line and those set during the failed attempt by John Lukens and his crew during the summer of 1763.

During their eighty-mile journey, the crew frequently encountered waterways. Chaining across small creeks was no problem; they just waded across. But measuring the width of the Nanticoke River, the first large waterway they encountered, presented a mathematical challenge, since the river was far wider than a Gunter's chain.

At the river's edge, Dixon set up an instrument called a Hadley's quadrant, which is used to measure angles between distant objects. Peering through the sight, he adjusted the quadrant so a mirror on the instrument reflected two separate objects on the opposite side of the river. A scale on the quadrant measured the angle created by Dixon and the two objects. Dixon used the angle in a mathematical computation called triangulation. The result provided him with the width of the river, which he added to their Gunter's chain measurements. While the Hadley's quadrant was sufficiently accurate for determining the width of a river, it was not an efficient tool for surveying the hilly terrain Dixon and Mason encountered along much of the Pennsylvania-Maryland boundary. Afterward, the surveyors crossed the river in canoes. Since canoes are a Native American watercraft and not used in England, this was probably Mason and Dixon's first canoe trip. Mason did not note whether either one of them attempted paddling.

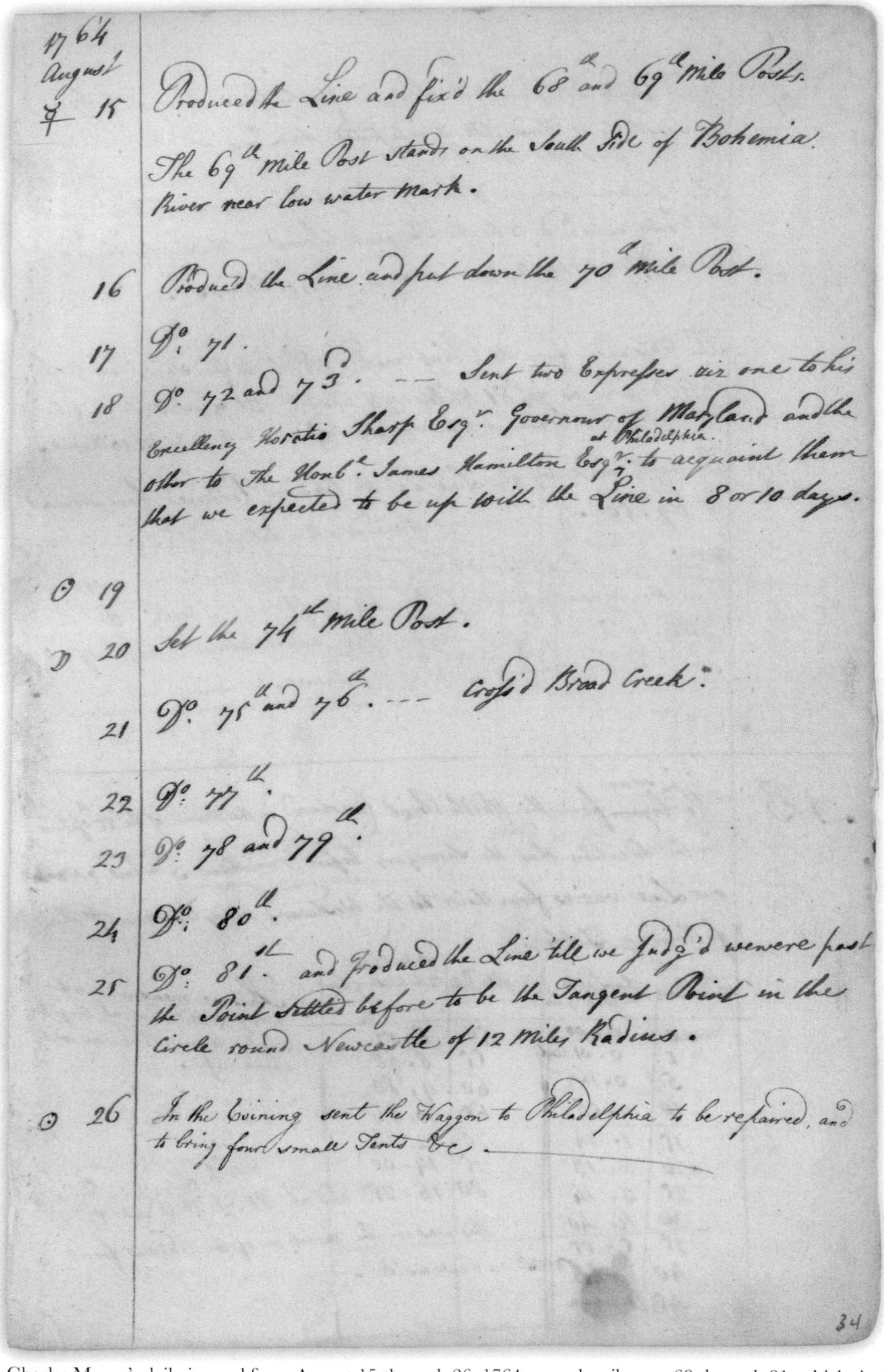

15 Produced the Line and fix'd the 68th and 69th Mile Posts.

The 69th Mile Post stands on the South Side of Bohemia River near low water mark.

16 Produced the Line and put down the 70th Mile Post.

17 Do. 71.

18 Do. 72 and 73. — Sent two Expresses viz one to his Excellency Horatio Sharp Esqr. Governour of Maryland and the other to the Honble. James Hamilton Esqr. at Philadelphia. to acquaint them that we expected to be up with the Line in 8 or 10 days.

19

20 Set the 74th Mile Post.

21 Do. 75th and 76th. — — — Cross'd Broad Creek.

22 Do. 77th.

23 Do. 78 and 79th.

24 Do. 80th.

25 Do. 81st. and Produced the Line 'till we Judg'd we were past the Point Settled before to be the Tangent Point in the Circle round Newcastle of 12 Miles Radius.

26 In the Evining sent the Waggon to Philadelphia to be repaired, and to bring four small Tents &c. —————————————

34

Charles Mason's daily journal from August 15 through 26, 1764, records mileposts 68 through 81, which signified the end of their eighty-mile-long straight line. On the 26th, he noted that a wagon needed repair.

By August 18, Mason and Dixon's straight line was seventy-three miles long. They sent express riders to the provincial governors to report that they expected to complete their line in eight to ten days. Wearily, they stopped after setting the eighty-first milepost, judging their position sufficiently north and west of the tangent point. Everyone was hot and exhausted. Makeshift repairs on shopworn equipment were no longer possible. McClean sent one of the wagons to Philadelphia for repair and directed the wagoner to bring four small tents when he returned.

Knowing their straight line was long enough—indeed, it extended farther north and west than the tangent point—Mason and Dixon's next job was to locate the actual tangent point. After doing so, they could begin the process of shifting their line eastward, where it could be correctly positioned and marked as the Tangent Line.

Trudging toward the New Castle Circle, crewmen cut back trees and shrubs until they found the mileposts, set by the 1760–1763 crew, that marked the twelve-mile radius from the courthouse in New Castle to the tangent point. The last post of the radius, which was set on the circle's circumference, was the tangent point. After they had revealed the posts, the crew cleared a vista westward from the tangent point to the straight line Mason and Dixon had just completed. Then the crew extended the radius of the New Castle Circle from the tangent point until it intersected Mason and Dixon's new line. They measured the distance with a Gunter's chain and found it to be 22.51 chains (almost 1,486 feet) long. Measuring this distance accurately was crucial for the calculations Mason would use to shift their new line over to the tangent point. And, like toppling dominos, that shift would help them determine the correct placement of all the other wooden mileposts between the tangent point and the Middle Point. (Later, the crew would physically move the posts.) To be certain that his calculations would be as accurate as possible, Mason insisted on double-checking the distance the crew had

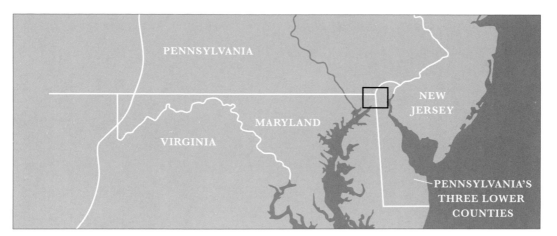

The black rectangle inset includes the beginning of the West Line.

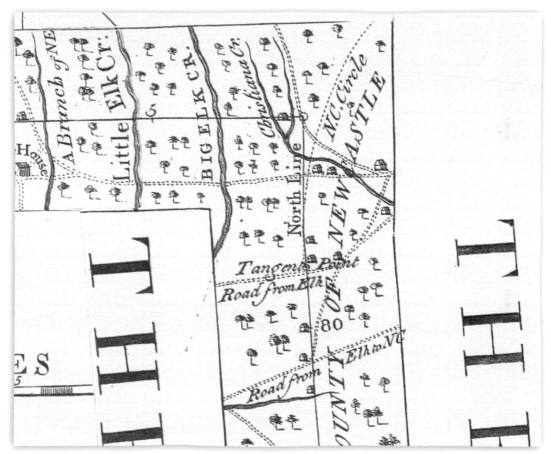

Dixon's map shows where the New Castle Circle touched the Tangent Line, creating the Tangent Point.

just chained: "To prove that the Chain Carriers had made no error in the measurement . . . I took a man with me, a few days after, and measured it myself: and made it within a Link of the same."

After nearly a week with no word about the fixed wagon or new tents, Mason and Dixon started back to the Middle Point. They were armed with crucial information. They knew their new line was straight. They knew the exact locations of the tangent point and the Middle Point. They knew the distance from the end of their straight line to the end of Lukens's 1763 survey line. They also knew the distance between the end of Lukens's line and the tangent point. And finally, they knew the locations of the 1763 five-mile markers. With this information, Mason calculated how much each of these markers would have to be moved eastward to be accurately set to create a true Tangent Line.

As they continued south, stories of the Pocomoke Swamp and its dark labyrinth of waterways that threaded through tangled shrubs and bear-filled woods piqued Mason and Dixon's curiosity about the mysterious land east of the Middle Point. One clear morning, they saddled their horses and trotted off to visit the swamp. The lush vegetation enchanted Mason: "There is the greatest quantity of Timber I ever saw: Above the Tallest Oak, Beech, Poplar, Hickory, Holly and Fir; Towers the lofty Cedar (without a Branch) 'till its ever green conical top seems to reach the clouds."

The closer to the Middle Point the crew got, the smaller the off-sets became between the old, incorrect line and the true Tangent Line, which ended only twenty-six inches to the west of the Middle Point. The next morning, beginning at this revised Middle Point, they headed back toward the tangent point. Along the way, they would take fresh measurements to double-check and tweak the accuracy of the Tangent Line and to ensure that the mileposts were set properly.

The meticulous measuring made the already tedious journey seem endless. It took the crew forty-four days to reach milepost 65. For three

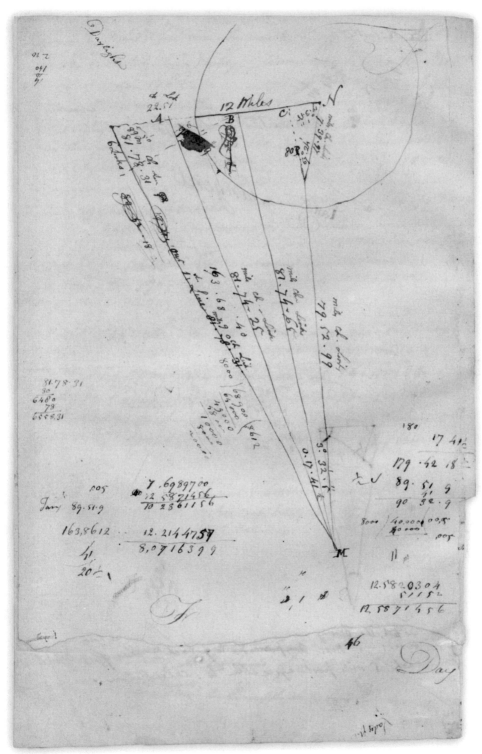

This diagram in Mason's journal includes the survey crew's measurements and some of the mathematical calculations he made to shift their eighty-mile-long line over to the tangent point.

McClean's account book of cash paid out (left page) and monies received (right page) for November 24, 1764, through April 6, 1765

Fol 3

The Hon'ble Commissioners of Maryland and Pennsylvania for settling the Lines of the said Provinces

1764 — To Moses McClean Steward   Dr   £ s d

Date	Entry	£	s	d
November 24	To Cash as p Ballance of s Accompts. Book L Fol (45)	24	9	7
	To Cash paid Thomas Thomas for 1 Turkey	0	3	
26	To Do paid Samuel Adair for Hay 2 days for 4 Horses	0	7	
	To Do paid Mary Thomas for 3 Quarts of milk a 3	0	0	9
	To Do paid Ebenezar Howel in Newark for Expences for Surveyors, Self, Waggoner &c	0	12	
	To Do paid Matthew Marine three days wages a 6/ p day from this day to the 28th Inclusive by Order of the Surveyors	0	18	
27	To Do paid Sarah Allison in Wilmington for Expen for self Waggoner & Horses over Night	0	12	
	To Do paid Peter Vandiver at Brandiwine Bridge for Do	0	1	
	To Do paid Matthew Kerlin for Expences	0	2	2
	To Do paid John Wethinson in Derby for Do	0	3	
	To Do paid Thomas James for Ferriage over Schuylkill	0	1	
28	To Do paid Mary Hall as p Voucher Book A No 1	0	11	
	To Do paid John Lukens as p Do Book A No 2	0	11	
	To Do paid Jacob Row as p Do Book A No 3	0	11	
	To Do paid Frederick Scheß for 3 days wages as Waggoner a 5/ p day Viz from the 26th of this Instant to this day Inclusive as p Do N A	0	15	
	To my wages as Steward a 12/6 p day from the 26th of this Instant to this day Inclusive being 3 day	1	17	9
	To Cash paid Christopher Rex as p Voucher N 5 Book A	0	9	
	To Do paid Frederick Scheß as p Do N 6 Book A	0	5	
1765				
January 23	To Do paid Arthur Broadas as p D No 7 Book D	14	15	
February 5	To Do paid Methuselah Evans as p D No 8 Do Do	9	0	
April 3d	To Do paid Lodowick Byman as p D No 9 Do Do	12	9	
	To Cash Transported to Fol (4)	68	16	

64	Contra Cr	L	S	D
ember 19	By Cash Received of Joseph Shippen Esqr	50	0	0
765				
il the 3	By Cash Received of Joseph Shippen Esqr by the Hands of Edward Shippen	400	0	0
6	By Do received of Mr Wescott for 3 old Brass Kettles	1	2	6
	By Cash Transported to Fol (4) L	451	2	6

days in November, work ground to a halt when thick fog made surveying impossible. During the downtime, Mason and Dixon met with the commissioners at George Town and updated them on their progress.

Finally, on November 10, the crew reached the eighty-mile mark. They found their line was sixteen feet nine inches east of the tangent point. Mason divided the difference proportionately over the entire length of the Tangent Line. By doing this, he could tell which of the mileposts, if any, were seriously out of position and, if so, have them reset. But the results satisfied him; none of the markers was set far enough off the Tangent Line to affect the line overall. The Tangent Line was as accurate as it could be.

Yet Mason insisted on one final accuracy check for the post he and Dixon had placed at the end of their Tangent Line. A line that is tangent to a circle is always perpendicular to the radius at the tangent point. Mason measured the angle between the end of their Tangent Line and the radius that extended from the belfry of the New Castle courthouse. Mason found "it was so near a right angle, that, on a mean from our Lines, the above mentioned Post is the true tangent Point."

On the eve of their first anniversary in America, Mason and Dixon were satisfied that they and their crew had successfully completed the Tangent Line. They'd done the impossible. They discharged the axmen and notified the governors of their results. The duo was delighted to hear that the equally satisfied boundary commissioners came to a resolution that "what we had done relating to the Lines should stand as finished."

As 1764 drew to a close, Mason and Dixon returned to John Harlan's home at the fork of the Brandywine, where they spent Christmas with their American friends.

Chapter Nine

THE WEST LINE

WITH CHRISTMAS and the 1765 New Year's festivities over, and the survey not scheduled to resume until spring, Mason and Dixon had plenty of time to relax at the Harlan home — to snooze, maybe ride the three miles to Joel Baily's house and head across the road with him to Martin's Tavern for a mug of ale. But Charles Mason was a man of action. Soon, colonial America and the promise of adventure beckoned. Mason heeded the call.

EXPLORING AMERICA

Despite the passage of a year, the Conestoga murders still weighed heavily on Charles Mason's mind. And Lancaster, where the tragedy had occurred, was less than thirty-five miles away. Mason felt compelled to visit the site: "What brought me here was my curiosity to see the place where was perpetrated last Winter the Horrid and inhuman murder of 26 Indians, men, Women and Children, leaving none alive to tell." (Mason was misinformed about the number of deaths.) The towns-people's lack of action that day disturbed him: "Strange it was that the Town though as large as most Market Towns in England, never offered to oppose them [the Paxton Boys], though it's more than probable they on request might have been assisted by a Company of his Majesties Troops who were then in the Town . . . no honor to them!" What Mason did, felt, and thought while visiting the town is a mystery. His journal is silent about that.

On his way back to Harlan's house, Mason detoured through Pechway (today Pequea), near the east bank of the Susquehanna River. There he crossed paths with Samuel Smith, who in 1736 had been the sheriff of Lancaster County. As new acquaintances do, they chatted and shared news. Mason told Smith about surveying the boundary line. And Smith regaled Mason with the hair-raising story of Thomas Cresap. Mason heard how "one Mr. Crisep defended his house as being in Maryland, with 14 men, which [Sheriff Smith] surrounded with about 55." Smith told Mason how Cresap and his friends "would not surrender (but kept firing out) till the House was set on fire, and one man in the House lost his life coming out." After conversing with Smith, Mason realized how important it was that the boundary line be firmly established.

In mid-February, his desire to see more of America unquenched, Mason put on his wig, pulled on his hat, and set off for New York City. His journey barely started before trouble nearly finished it.

After spending the night at the home of Moses and Sarah McClean, Mason prepared to cross the Delaware River. Choosing a place where the river was about a quarter of a mile wide, Mason reined his horse down the riverbank and onto the ice. Partway across, a loud crack beneath the horse's hooves froze Mason's blood harder than the ice. Horse and rider plunged into the cold water. Watching his horse flounder, Mason feared the worst. Fortunately, the horse regained its footing and, without serious harm, the two safely reached shore.

After leaving New York, Mason rode south through New Jersey, where trouble found him yet again:

> Met some boys just come out of a Quaker meeting House as if the Devil had been with them. I could by no means get my Horse by them. I gave the Horse a light blow on the Head with my whip which brought him to the ground as if shot dead. I over his Head, my hat one-way wig another and whip another, fine sport for the boys. However I got up as did my Horse after some time and I led him by the Meeting House, (the Friends pouring out) very serene, as if all had been well.

The next day, with wounded pride and a sore hip, Mason remained in bed. Two days later, he again crossed the Delaware River—this time by boat—and joined Dixon in lodgings a few miles from Mr. Bryan's field and the Post Marked West. There the two men prepared a precise plan for running the Western Line.

THE WESTWARD TREK

One star, Delta Ursae Minoris, had steered the course for the Tangent Line. Mason now chose five key stars as the guides for the West Line. They are commonly known as Vega, Deneb, Sadr, Delta Cygni, and Capella. These stars are found in the constellations Lyra, Cygnus, and Auriga. Using this many stars would firmly anchor the team to the West Line's latitude, which gradually curves around the earth.

THE FUSS ABOUT STAMPS

*W*HILE MASON AND DIXON *were in America, they had front-row seats for observing some of the earliest dissatisfactions that would slowly push thirteen American colonies on the road to rebellion. In taverns, at inns, and at the Harlans' house, the surveyors certainly would have heard discussions about stamps. In every newspaper, they would have read articles about the Stamp Act. On June 20, 1765, the* Pennsylvania Gazette *carried word from Annapolis that "the Stamp Act is to take Place in America, on All Saints Day, the First of November next." Ministers preached against the new law from their pulpits. And on November first, that day on "which the fatal and never-to-be-forgotten Stamp-Act" was intended to take effect, the bells in many colonial American towns tolled long and solemnly. Crowds demonstrated in the streets. Outraged merchants fussed and fumed.*

What was the fuss over stamps?

First of all, they were not postage stamps. The act levied a tax on all American colonists for every piece of printed paper they used: newspapers, printed pamphlets, legal documents, land deeds, licenses, even playing cards. The paper used for these materials had to come directly from England, and a revenue stamp would be impressed into each sheet of paper. The amount of the tax — the cost of the stamp — varied according to the intended use of the paper and ranged from two pence up to six pounds. Parchment for a university degree cost two pounds; papers for court documents could cost from three pence to six pounds. The money collected would help pay the costs of stationing British troops along the boundary of the Appalachian Mountains, the border of Indian Territory. With the Stamp Act, Parliament reasoned, colonists would be paying, at least partially, for their own protection and defense.

The British government levied a tax on American colonists each time they used a piece of printed paper. A stamp, like the one shown here, noting the amount of money due, was impressed into the paper.

In response to the act's passage, colonists held a Stamp Act Congress in New York City in October 1765. Twenty-seven delegates from nine colonies — Connecticut, Delaware, Maryland, Massachusetts, New Jersey, New York, Pennsylvania, Rhode Island, and South Carolina — attended. The colonists objected to the new tax on important grounds: because none of the American colonies were able to choose members of Parliament to represent them, the British government had no right to levy taxes on them. In other words, they were being subjected to "taxation without representation."

The Stamp Act Congress declared that after January 1, 1766, Americans would resolve "not to buy any goods, wares, or merchandizes, of any person or persons whatsoever, that shall be shipped from Great-Brittain . . . unless the Stamp Act shall be repealed." Further, the congress observed that British trade would suffer if American merchants refused to import goods from England.

Angry colonists protested the Stamp Act in various ways, including creating this parody of the official stamp.

The widespread protests of colonial people and the resolutions of the Stamp Act Congress gained the support of several members of Parliament. On February 21, 1766, Parliament soundly voted to repeal the Stamp Act, and the king gave his approval on March 18, 1766. Colonial activists had succeeded in their quest to repeal the Stamp Act. Mason and Dixon were thus on hand to observe the planting of one of the important seeds that grew into the American Revolution. "No Taxation Without Representation" became one of the battle cries when, in 1776, colonial Americans created new political boundaries by declaring themselves a country separate from England.

Beginning the West Line was as trouble-plagued as Mason's winter break had been. Driving rains completely shut down operations on departure day, March 19. Gamely, the surveyors had managed to set one marker a half mile from the starting point. After that, dripping wet and muddy from head to toe, they called it a day.

The next day, weather hit them with two punches: plummeting temperatures and steady snow. When it stopped, two feet ten inches of snow blanketed the ground. Deep drifts barricaded the wagons. Five days passed before Jonathan Cope and William Darby, two of the crew's most experienced chain carriers, dared travel the road from their homes in the Three Lower Counties to the Brandywine. All the team could do was wait. Mason and Dixon wanted to reach the bank of the Susquehanna River before mid-May. They hoped the weather delays wouldn't completely derail their schedule.

The westward trek finally began on April 5. While hints of spring touched the air, enough chill remained to make cheeks and fingers tingle. Patches of melting snow slickened the ground and slowed wagon wheels. Eight days later—twelve miles and nine chains from the Post Marked West—tent keeper Alexander McClean, Moses's nineteen-year-old brother (at least five McClean brothers worked on the West Line), helped set up tents in the line's first camp. The tents' linen fibers were spun in such a way that if a tent got wet, the fibers slightly untwisted and swelled, closing up the tiny openings between individual strands and making the tent more watertight. Some other tents used by the team may have been lined with wool. Like linen fibers, wool fibers expand when wet. In damp spring weather, the expanded wool would have reduced the amount of cold air that seeped through the tent walls. The surveyors did not describe the shape of the tents used by the crew, but it is reasonable to suppose the men had wedge-shaped or A-shaped tents similar to those used by the military. These tents, measuring six feet by six feet by six feet, weighed from fifteen to twenty pounds and provided sleeping quarters and shelter for up to six men. As the bosses, Mason and Dixon may have used a larger wedge tent or a small marquee tent, which would have weighed two, or even three, times as much. All the tents were supported by at least two upright wooden tentpoles, as well as a long ridgepole. These long, heavy poles were awkward to transport and unwieldy to handle during setup.

While Alexander McClean hammered tent pegs, full-time cooks Leven Hickman and Charles Platt unpacked kettles and knives, lit a fire, and prepared supper. Mason and Dixon discussed the past week's work with John Harlan, who had joined the crew as an instrument bearer, and asked Cope and Darby to return to Mr. Bryan's field in the morning to get the zenith sector. Optimistically, on April 30, the surveyors sent express messages to the commissioners saying they would reach the Susquehanna River in twelve days. The pressure was on.

Everyone settled in to camp, knowing the surveyors' eyes would be glued to the skies for the next two weeks to confirm their course. Because the earth's surface curves, Mason could plot the true course for a distance of only ten to eleven miles. So every time the crew had traveled about that distance, Mason spent time stargazing. After he confirmed that they were still properly on the latitude of the West Line ($39°43'18.2''$ N)—or making corrections if they weren't—Dixon could resume chaining the next day confident that he was on course.

On May 11, at 26 miles 3 chains 93 links, the survey crew reached the east bank of the mighty Susquehanna River and made camp, exactly on schedule. At night, Mason stargazed. In the daytime, Dixon measured the width of the Susquehanna with the Hadley's quadrant.

On May 25, as evening approached, Mason was hard at work across the river from camp. As he shifted his gaze from the task at hand, he noticed massive dark clouds on the horizon. Thunder grumbled low, and lightning flashed. Nerves on edge, Mason hurried to a boat:

> [As] I was returning from the other Side of the River, and at the distance of about 1.5 Mile the Lightning fell in perpendicular streaks, (about a foot in breadth to appearance) from the cloud to the ground. This was the first Lightning I ever saw in streaks continued without the least break through the whole, all the way from the Cloud to the Horizon.

Even though the fierce spectacle awed him, as soon as his boat touched shore, he hustled away from the water and safely out of the lightning's path.

Having completed the survey as far as the Susquehanna River, the entire crew trudged back east, toward the Post Marked West, double-checking the accuracy of the set mileposts along the way, and then headed south. By June 1, they reached the tangent point, where they surveyed a short line called the North Line. This line, 5 miles 1 chain and 50 links long, extended north along the meridian from the tangent point to the point where it intersected the West Line in a meadow owned by Captain John Singleton. Surveying the North Line completed the eastern boundary, where Maryland, Pennsylvania, and the Lower Counties (Delaware) come together. Mason and Dixon marked the spot with a post that had a *W* carved on its west side and an *N* on its north side.

Pleased with the crew's results, the commissioners decided it was time to set some of the permanent boundary stones, which had been shipped from England. Among the seven stones placed were one at the tangent point and one at the intersection of the North and West Lines.

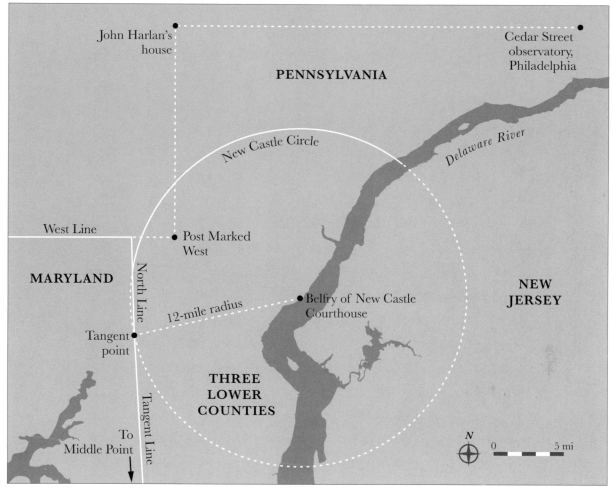

When combined, the Tangent Line and the North Line completed the eastern boundary between the land owned by the Calverts and that owned by the Penns. The solid white lines are boundary lines.

Afterward, the commissioners again sent the surveyors west to continue the line "in the same manner [from] the River Susquehanna . . . as far as the country is inhabited." The farther west the survey crew traveled, the more rugged the countryside became. In some places, trees grew so closely together that a person with outstretched arms couldn't walk without bumping against a tree trunk. The crew chopped down trees to clear Dixon's vista and pressed steadily on.

No matter how carefully Moses McClean managed the crew and livestock, occasional problems cropped up. During a weeklong stop in mid-July, two horses wandered off. As he had five years earlier, McClean paid an express rider ten shillings to ride to Philadelphia and place an ad for the missing horses in the newspaper.

While McClean dealt with missing horses, the surveyors watched the five key stars and discovered that the line had drifted too far south by 56 feet (85 links). They corrected their position and continued westward. As the dog days of summer passed from July into August, sweat dripped from the axmen's faces. At noon on August 8, a little over seventy-one miles from the Post Marked West, the laboring crew finally received some respite from the heat—though unfortunately, it was in the form of a fierce thunderstorm. Hail pelted the tents and shredded leaves from trees. Amazed by the size of the hailstones, Mason grabbed a large one and measured it before it melted. It was "one inch and six tenths in Length, one inch two tenths in breadth and half an inch thick."

Meanwhile, back in England, the Penns and Lord Baltimore grew impatient, despite news from Maryland's governor Sharpe that the whole line would not likely be finished in 1765. They read copies of the minutes of the Boundary Commission meetings, so they knew that progress had been made. Even so, the survey seemed to be taking a long time. The proprietors hoped the commission wouldn't have to be extended for yet another year. Each day added, every delay reported, only increased the proprietors' frustration over the mounting costs of an already expensive undertaking. But, as Governor Sharpe explained in a letter dated July 10, 1765, "the Taking [of] frequent Observations with their Sector is exceeding tedious & retards them sometimes for near three Weeks together I do not expect they will this Summer extend the Line by many Miles." The commissioners wished the survey would end as much as the proprietors did. Traveling back and forth to boundary-line meetings was arduous and disruptive. There was, however, no way to hurry the stars.

Surveying the West Line was not all about computations. The commissioners had also encouraged Mason and Dixon to engage the colonists along the way. The commissioners had done so, realizing that keeping people informed was a good way to allay fears and anger about property issues. Phinehas Davidson, who lived near milepost 86, would have chatted with the surveyors, since their line might easily cross his property. He must have told them he was a pretty good cook, as Moses McClean later hired him. By the end of August 1765, the crew included more than forty men, many of whom worked as axmen. One of them was Phinehas Harlan, John and Sarah's twenty-four-year-old son. Working for Mason and Dixon was a good way for him to save some money for his future — his sweetheart, Elizabeth, whom he hoped someday to marry, was waiting for him back at home.

A local resident visited the surveyors' camp near milepost 95 on Sunday, September 22. Since it was the crew's day off, the surveyors accepted his offer to go spelunking. Dixon, whose father operated a coal mine, was very familiar with large holes in the ground. But this cave, the resident assured him, was quite different. Dixon and Mason saddled up for the six-mile journey.

Carrying lanterns, the men ducked as they entered the cool, damp cave. After passing through the arched mouth, they straightened. "Immediately there opens a room," Mason wrote, "45 yards in length, 40 in breadth and 7 or 8 in height. (Not one pillar to support nature's arch)." The dim light of their flickering lanterns revealed formations that astonished them: it was like being inside a cathedral. "On the sidewalls are drawn by the Pencil of Time, with the tears of the Rocks: The imitation of Organ, Pillar, Columns and Monuments of a Temple." Indeed, their guide told them that during the winter, local residents attended

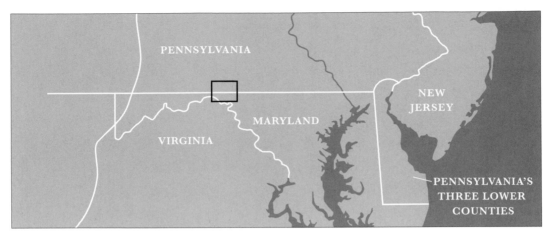

The black rectangle inset includes the area that surrounds mileposts 105–115 of the West Line.

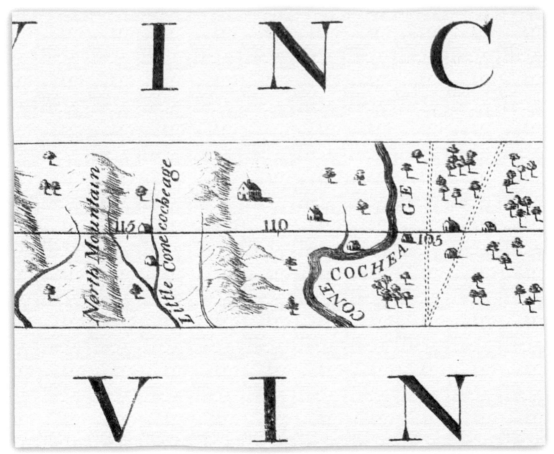

Dixon's map shows the crew crossed rivers, creeks, and mountains along this stretch of the West Line.

church services inside the cave. Profoundly moved, Mason described the hushed atmosphere of the large chamber as "Striking its Visitants with a strong and melancholy reflection: That such is the abodes of the Dead: Thy inevitable doom, O stranger; Soon to be numbered as one of them." Further exploration of the cave brought them to "a fine river of water" and "other rooms, but not so large as the first."

The next Sunday, Mason and Dixon forded the Potomac River and crossed into Virginia, where they saw a log fort—a reminder of the ever-present troubles in the wilderness—and a tavern. As was fairly common at the time, Mason and Dixon were known for enjoying wine, ale, and other alcoholic beverages. Their expense reports included receipts for wineglasses and liquor. What's more, frontier taverns—busy places visited by both local residents and travelers—were the best places to go to catch up on news of all sorts.

By the end of the first week of October, at milepost 117, near North Mountain, they'd reached the end of the survey for that season. They remained camped there for three weeks, stargazing and confirming the accuracy of the West Line. With an ax, Dixon chopped a mark in a tree whose position had been precisely noted with relation to the positions of several stars at a certain time. The next season, Mason planned to recheck the line's accuracy using the positions of those stars and the marked tree.

Having been instructed that the West Line should not cross the meandering Potomac River, the surveyors asked local resident Captain Evan Shelby to hike with them to the top of North Mountain and point out the river's path. After showing them how the river looped about two miles south of the line, Shelby pointed out Allegheny Mountain, which the surveyors judged "by its appearance to be about 50 miles (in) distance in the direction of our Line." The view from the summit of North Mountain was the surveyors' last westward view of the season.

The next day, with winter on the horizon, Mason and Dixon packed the instruments and "left them (not in the least damaged to our knowledge) at Captain Shelby's." The crew began its return to the Susquehanna River, checking their offsets along the way. On November 8, at the settlement of Peach Bottom Ferry, Mason and Dixon discharged all hands and left for the town of York, where they met with the boundary-line commissioners for nearly a week. Did the commissioners celebrate on November 15, the second anniversary of the surveyors' arrival in America? Or did they fill the surveyors' ears with the proprietors' complaints about time and money? The commissioners definitely piled on further instructions: proceed at once to the Middle Point, at the southern end of the Tangent Line, and supervise the setting of fifty boundary stones.

In early December, Mason and Dixon arrived at the home of John Twiford, on the Nanticoke River. They had come to know Twiford well when they'd surveyed the Tangent Line. They waited nearly two weeks at his house before a barge delivered twenty boundary stone markers to Twiford's wharf. Another barge delivered an additional thirty stones on the bank of the Choptank River, midway along the Tangent Line. Wagons carried the stones and men hired by Reverend John Ewing, one of the Pennsylvania commissioners, along the Tangent Line as the men dug holes and set the stones. On January 1, 1766, with all fifty stones set, Mason and Dixon released the crew for the cold season and settled down for the winter with the Harlans at Brandywine Creek. With much work still to be done, the lords proprietors had no choice but to extend the boundary commission another year to December 31, 1766. Surely *that* would be enough time.

SET IN STONE

CREATING a permanently marked boundary line was critical. Mason and Dixon used boundary stones similar to those used by the crew that had surveyed the Transpeninsular Line several years earlier. The boundary stones were taken from limestone quarries on the Isle of Portland, in the English Channel along southwestern England. The stones are rectangular pillars, with each stone twelve inches across and the top tapering to a shallow pyramid. They were 3½ to 4½ feet tall and weighed 300 to 600 pounds. Some of the stones, called crown stones, had the Calvert

and Penn families' coats of arms carved on opposite sides; these were placed at five-mile intervals. Others were simply inscribed with a capital M on the side that faced Maryland and a P on the side facing Pennsylvania; these marked each mile between the crown stones. In a letter to Cecilius Calvert, Governor Sharpe estimated that the team would need between fifty and sixty crown stones and about two hundred regular mile markers. The stones, shipped from England as ship ballast, were unloaded onto wharves in Maryland, where they were shipped inland by barge and/or wagon.

The crown stone on the far left, seen full-length, shows the Penn family coat of arms, which would have faced Pennsylvania. The crown stone on the near left shows the Calvert coat of arms, facing Maryland.

Chapter Ten

CONTINUING WEST

DURING THE WINTER BREAK, Jeremiah Dixon, who'd spent part of the time in Philadelphia, met with boundary commissioners in Maryland to report on the team's plan for the new season and the money they'd need to carry it out. By the end of March 1766, Mason, Dixon, Darby, and Cope had assembled at Captain Shelby's house, at milepost 117 near North Mountain, where the survey had halted the previous year. They star-checked Dixon's notched tree, made some corrections to the West Line's direction, and began chaining. The terrain made for slow, strenuous work. After crossing a creek, Mason, Dixon, and the crew climbed the steep flank of North Mountain. It took them seven days to extend the line two miles.

Slowed work wasn't their only problem. As with the previous year, unpredictable spring weather—this time snow and six days of rain—stranded an increasingly impatient Moses McClean miles away. Chomping at the bit to deliver the wagons loaded with tents and supplies to the survey crew, McClean nevertheless knew that waiting until the ground dried would save time in the long run. Wagon wheels clogged and weighted with thick mud would add to the horses' burden, and all wagoners hated digging out wheels mired in mud. McClean and the well-stocked wagons finally rolled into sight on April 14, 1766. While he knew that Mason and Dixon would be glad to see him, he also knew that they would not be pleased to learn that he'd run out of cash.

Money from Lord Baltimore and the Penns financed the boundary-line survey. A signed commission stipulated that Mason's and Dixon's wages would be paid upon completion of the survey. But every item or service incurred while running the survey had to be paid for. Maryland and Pennsylvania boundary-line commissioners held the purse strings for these expenses, which were many: axmen, carpenters, food, wagons, horses, hay, oats, candles, tents, ink powder, lodging, ferry crossings, and a haystack damaged while running the Tangent Line. Even a silk handkerchief and a coffin were included in one of the expense reports. Periodically, the commissioners dispensed funds. In December 1764, Joseph Shippen, Pennsylvania's provincial secretary, sent Moses McClean fifty pounds; four months later, he sent an additional four hundred pounds.

Continuing the West Line without funds was unthinkable. The surveyors sent an express letter to Governor Sharpe requesting more funds, noting that "on the whole . . . we have received 615 pounds more of the Proprietors of Pensilvania than of Lord Baltimore. We expect you will please to send 6 or 700 pounds that Mr. McLane may receive it at Frederick Town (as you proposed) the 24th of this month, we having no Cash to proceed with." Fortunately, McClean was good at obtaining credit from his suppliers, so the continuation of the West Line was not delayed. And Sharpe did, eventually, send money.

Despite sporadic snow flurries, the crew pressed westward. The horses had little trouble hauling the wagons through a few inches of snow.

But they halted shortly after milepost 134, defeated by the steep east flank of Sideling Hill. On foot, Dixon and the chain carriers struggled to measure accurately and even to remain upright while threading their way through oak and hickory trees to the summit, which crested at more than 2,300 feet. On the way down, they were forced to take sideways steps and grab small trees to keep from falling or sliding dangerously downhill. Safely at the bottom, 140 miles 15 chains 76 links from the Post Marked West, Mason and Dixon ordered the zenith sector brought from Captain Shelby's house. There, with "oak and hickory buds just breaking into Leaf," Mason and Dixon spent three weeks observing the stars and making calculations.

From May 19 to June 5, 1766, roller-coaster geography between mileposts 140 and 165 taxed the crew to its limits. As soon as they climbed down one mountain, another faced them. They measured up and down Town Hill, Ragged Mountain, Little Warrior Mountain, Great Warrior Mountain, Flintstone Mountain, Evitts Creek Mountain, Nobbley Mountain, Will's Creek Mountain, and the little Allegheny Mountain, all of which had elevations as high as Sideling Hill. On June 9, when Mason and Dixon again set up the zenith sector, everyone was exhausted but glad. They had reached the end of the road for the West Line.

On Saturday, June 14, Mason hiked to the top of Savage Mountain and gazed westward. The mountaintop where he stood was one in the chain that formed the "Boundary between the Natives and strangers; in these parts of his Britanic Majesties Collonies." King George III's Royal Proclamation of 1763 temporarily forbade colonists from homesteading in that area, declaring it Indian Territory. Yet colonists in the area had told Mason that the fertile lands on the far side of the boundary were "the best of any in the known parts of North America" and that "The Rivers abound with variety of fish, and quantity almost increditable." Mason, a fisherman, longed to test the truth of the colonists' claims.

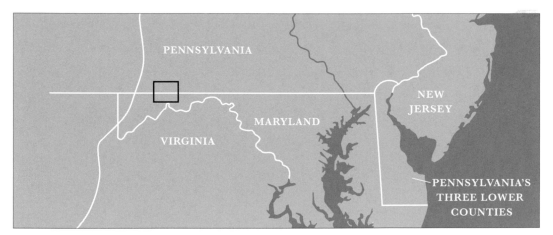

The black rectangle inset includes the area that surrounds mileposts 145–160 of the West Line.

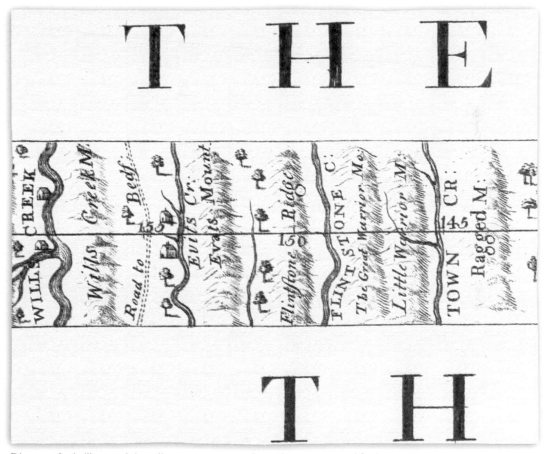

Dixon perfectly illustrated the roller-coaster topography as the crew surveyed farther west.

As Mason looked out at the creeks and rivers on either side of Savage Mountain, he realized that he could see the Eastern Continental Divide. The vast American countryside truly touched Mason: "From the solitary tops of these mountains," he wrote, "the Eye gazes round with pleasure; filling the mind with adoration to that pervading spirit that made them."

A CRUSHING DEFEAT

*F*ROM 1754 TO 1763, *war between English and French forces raged along colonial America's western and northern frontiers. Because the Iroquois confederation and some other native peoples allied themselves with the French, the war became known as the French and Indian War.*

When he arrived in the colonies in 1755, General Edward Braddock, England's commander in chief, planned to capture Fort Duquesne, built and held by the French, in western Pennsylvania. (The city of Pittsburgh now occupies the site.) One of Braddock's aides-de-camp was a twenty-three-year-old Virginian named George Washington.

To begin his campaign, General Braddock needed horses and wagons. Without them, his troops and artillery couldn't get to Fort Cumberland, which was built in 1754 by Maryland's militia and lay halfway to Fort Duquesne. Benjamin Franklin, postmaster general of Pennsylvania, rallied to Braddock's aid, appealing in a newspaper ad to his fellow colonists' sense of loyalty to king and country. His plea garnered 150 wagons and 500 horses for the cause. A second appeal yielded forty-one wagonloads of oats and Indian corn to feed the horses.

With almost 2,100 men — a combination of British regulars and colonial militia — assembled at Fort Cumberland, Braddock was ready for the march on Fort Duquesne. But bringing provisions and artillery along with his troops was impossible without a road. Following the path of an old Indian trail, six hundred of Braddock's men cut a road, twelve feet wide, through the wilderness. Slowly, Braddock's troops advanced.

On their way to Fort Duquesne in 1755, General Braddock's army was ambushed by French and Indian forces. Years later, during the Revolutionary War, General George Washington borrowed many of the Indians' battle tactics.

On July 9, two or three miles from Fort Duquesne, French and Indian forces hiding behind rocks and trees attacked Braddock's army. The British regulars, unfamiliar with this kind of guerrilla warfare, panicked. George Washington later described the battle:

Our numbers consisted of about 1300 well arm'd Men, chiefly Regular's, who were immediately struck with such a deadly Panick, that nothing but confusion and disobedience of order's prevail'd amongst them. . . . In short the dastardly behaviour of the English soldier's expos'd all those who were inclin'd to do their duty to almost certain Death; and at length, in despight of every [officer's] effort to the contrary, [the Regulars] broke and run as Sheep before the Hounds, leaving the Artillery, Ammunition, Provisions, and every individual thing we had with us a prey to the Enemy.

General Braddock, mortally wounded in the chest, was carried from the battlefield in a wagon as the remaining British troops fled. Almost nine hundred men were killed, wounded, or left on the battlefield. Washington and others blamed as many as two-thirds of the company's deaths on shots fired by the panicked regulars — in modern language, friendly fire.

WITH AXES SWINGING

Even though Mason, Dixon, and their team had reached the end of the West Line, their job was by no means finished. The axmen sharpened their blades and chopped, calling out as trees tumbled. The men hauled brush and dragged tree trunks until they had cleared an eight-foot-wide vista along the parallel of the West Line. It was a boundary line no one could miss.

On Sunday, June 22, 1766, while the crew rested, Mason and Dixon journeyed back in time by visiting Fort Cumberland, located at the confluence of Will's Creek and the Potomac River. Commissioner Peters had described the log fort as a "dismal inhospitable Place."

As his horse trotted along a stretch of the road that had been cleared by General Braddock's men, Mason couldn't help but think of the tragic battle—how almost exactly eleven years earlier, the road he was riding on had been crowded with wounded and dying men. How ironic and sad, Mason wrote, that Braddock "made through the desert a path, himself to pass; and never; never to return." While Fort Cumberland, "beautifully situated on a rising ground," looked good from a distance, when the surveyors went inside, they saw that it was in bad repair. While the French and English had officially made peace three years earlier, Mason and Dixon knew firsthand—from stories heard in taverns, from colonists they'd met, and from visiting the site of the Conestoga massacre—that violent incidents between colonists and native people still occurred.

The next day, the surveyors were back on the line as the axmen resumed work clearing the vista to the Post Marked West, a job that occupied them fully through the summer. Yet Mason still found time to investigate the natural world. Hickory trees grew abundantly in the region, and although the nuts weren't ripe in July, the trees' spicy aroma scented the air. He marveled at the size of the hickory leaves and "measured three leaves on one Stem . . . each of which was 17 inches in length and 12 inches in breadth."

The crew completed the West Line vista when it intersected the North Line. On September 30, the surveyors discharged all hands. Summarizing their achievements, Mason noted that he and Dixon periodically stood on hillcrests that commanded a view of fifteen or twenty miles east or west and happily found the West Line easily visible and nicely conforming to the parallel of latitude. If they celebrated their achievement in any way, no letters or documents survive to tell about it.

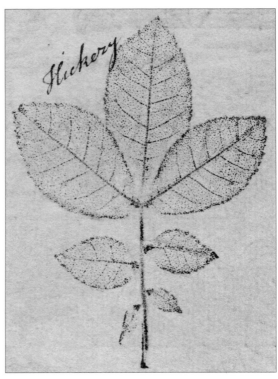

This hickory leaf print (shown close to actual size) was made by Joseph Breintnall circa 1730. This leaf was much smaller than the ones Mason measured.

With no boundary-line meetings scheduled until the end of October, Mason and Dixon engaged themselves in another task. The Royal Society, the organization that had sponsored their 1761 transit of Venus expedition, hired them to measure the length of a degree of latitude in America. In Europe, French scientists had calculated the length at 69.5 miles. In the scientific quest to determine Earth's precise shape, knowing if this length varied in different places on Earth's surface was critical. In completing this task, Mason and Dixon would be literally and scientifically charting new territory.

With permission from the proprietors of both provinces, they departed for the Middle Point, back in southern Maryland, accompanied by three experienced crewmen. Choosing the Middle Point saved time, since star positions and land distances had already been measured and marked there. Even so, they spent two weeks monitoring ten stars with the zenith sector: timing the arc-shaped path of each one and recording the angles formed between the horizon, the surveyors, and the star. Mason used the information to reconfirm the exact latitude of the Middle Point.

Working at night, Dixon and one of the crewmen chained a straight line exactly one mile long north along the meridian. In the daytime, they measured the distance, at a right angle, from the end of the one-mile-long line to the Tangent Line. (The Tangent Line extended in a northwest direction, not straight north.) Later, they would collect additional information at the Stargazer's Stone and remeasure the Tangent Line. The combined data from these three endeavors would eventually enable them to calculate the length of a degree of latitude. But until they had that additional information, they had done all they could do on the Royal Society's project. Afterward, Mason and Dixon rode to New Castle County, where one of the Pennsylvania commissioners met and instructed them "to proceed immediately to set 100 Stones (one at each mile) in the [West] Line."

During November, men hauled boundary stones to the wooden mile markers. One commissioner from each province accompanied them to make sure that the stones were accurately placed and did not favor a particular colony. Mason and Dixon passed the anniversary of their third year in America reviewing their accomplishments in meetings with the commissioners. The lines had been surveyed. All the boundary stones for the Tangent Line were in place, as were those along the North Line. Along the West Line, stones stood at every mile for sixty-five miles, except at the sixty-fourth mile, where there was no stone due to unfavorable geography. Mason and Dixon's job for the Penns and Lord Calvert was done. Or was it?

Chapter Eleven

DANGEROUS TERRITORY

INSTEAD OF OFFERING Mason and Dixon tickets back to England, the commissioners had new instructions for more work. The first job was surveying an eleven-mile line from the Post Marked West east to the Delaware River. Although this line wasn't part of the boundary line, knowing its length would allow the commissioners to calculate exactly how far west Pennsylvania extended. The king's charter to William Penn defined the westernmost limit of the province as five degrees of longitude west of the Delaware River. This job took Mason and Dixon slightly less than a week.

The second job, however, was huge: return to the westernmost end of the West Line and continue the line until it reached the spot exactly five degrees longitude west of the Delaware River, as had been established in the charter. Accomplishing this job meant crossing the boundary into land under the jurisdiction of the Six Nations. Under the king's 1763 proclamation, English colonists were not supposed to settle there, and traveling through this territory without the confederacy's consent could cause misunderstandings that might have violent consequences. So Governors John Penn and Horatio Sharpe wrote letters to Indian agent William Johnson, who agreed to ask the Six Nations' leaders for their consent, which the governors hoped would arrive by March or early April 1767. Mason and Dixon realized that this meant more work, more delays, and more time in America as they awaited news from Johnson at the Harlans' house. Meanwhile, anticipating the Indians' consent, the lords proprietors had extended the boundary-line commission for yet another year, through December 31, 1767.

A DIFFERENT SORT OF SURVEY

Within days of their arrival at the Harlans' house, the surveyors used the zenith sector to observe the same stars they'd recently observed at the Middle Point, collecting more of the star-related data they would need to compute the length of a degree of latitude. But in January 1767, Mason and Dixon also began gathering information of a different sort. Their new observations, made at the request of the Royal Society, would help scientists understand how—or if—gravity was affected by latitude. They used two pendulum clocks. One belonged to the proprietors and had already been used many times during the survey. The other clock had been made by John Shelton, a famous English clockmaker, and was shipped to them by Nevil Maskelyne of the Royal Society, who had used it to time the transit of Venus on Saint Helena Island. Mason and Dixon recorded the time shown on both clocks at least twice daily, noting any differences. Maskelyne also sent two thermometers made by John Bird, the man who had made the zenith sector. Twice daily, Dixon and Mason used these to record the temperature of the air inside and outside the observatory tent. All this data would help support or refute a scientific hypothesis.

Scientists of the day hypothesized that Earth's gravitational force varied with latitude—so that, for example, the gravitational force along Pennsylvania's latitude was different from that along Saint Helena's latitude. They hoped the Shelton clock would help prove it. Each swing of the clock's pendulum advanced a set of gears that in turn moved the clock's hands. Earth's gravity pulled on the swinging pendulum. If gravity's force was stronger in the clock's current location than it had been in its previous location, the pendulum's movement would be slightly slower and the clock would lose time. If gravity's force was lower, the pendulum would swing more freely and the clock would gain time.

The Shelton clock's pendulum was made of brass; the proprietors' clock had a walnut pendulum. The brass pendulum would shrink or expand minutely in response to cold or heat, which could affect the rate at which it swung.

The Shelton pendulum clock used by Mason and Dixon in their observatory in Harlan's garden. The base and pedestal were added later.

On New Year's Day, the outside temperature plummeted to 22° below zero Fahrenheit. Conditions inside the tent, at 9° below zero Fahrenheit, weren't much better. The metal transit and equal altitude instrument was so cold that "the immediate touch of the Brass was like patting one's Fingers against the points of Pins and Needles." On January 27, three days of freezing rain coated Mason and Dixon's world with ice. Although sunlight sparkled magically on the ice, "the limbs of the Trees broke in a surprising manner, with the weight of clear Ice upon them." Despite dangerous falling branches, the two men faithfully recorded times and temperatures.

With observations completed at the end of February, Mason packed the Shelton clock and sent it, along with all their time and temperature records, to the Royal Society in England. There, scientists would compare the data with similar records kept by Maskelyne, using the same clock, on Saint Helena. Mason and Dixon's observations did help prove the hypothesis. It was later confirmed that gravity had indeed affected the rate of the pendulum's speed in Pennsylvania, causing a variation from the rates observed at Saint Helena.

Even as the Shelton clock stopped ticking, time marched forward. The commissioners, surveyors, and provincial proprietors all waited impatiently for word to arrive from William Johnson and the Indians.

DELICATE NEGOTIATIONS

William Johnson was a longtime resident of the province of New York. He lived on land near Mohawk territory, spoke Mohawk, and was in a common-law marriage with Molly Brant, a Mohawk woman. At Six Nations council meetings, he dressed in Mohawk clothing and participated in ceremonial dances. Johnson understood and respected cultural boundaries that most colonists did not.

Acquiring permission for Mason and Dixon to survey beyond the colonies' borders would require patience and diplomacy. First, Johnson insisted that "all the Chief Sackems [sic] and principal Warriors of the Six Nations" be present at the council meeting during which he would request permission. He estimated that assembling the large group at a place conveniently located and supplying them with presents would cost about five hundred pounds in New York currency (equivalent to three hundred pounds in British currency), an expense the lords proprietors of the two provinces would have to bear. Additionally, plans being developed in London regarding a different boundary line between England's colonies and Indian territory had become mired in governmental meetings. This proposed line was completely unrelated to the West Line, but Johnson had to allay the Indians' suspicions that Mason and Dixon's survey was connected with the stalled boundary line under discussion in London. Furthermore, he needed to schedule the council meeting before the Indians' hunting season began.

Delayed by unusual spring flooding, the council meeting didn't occur until May 8 to 11, 1767. As protocol required, Johnson began by presenting strings of wampum to the Indians. Wampum presented during a council meeting was not being used as money. Instead, it signaled that a matter of importance was being discussed and considered. The three strings Johnson offered signified the beginning of a time for discussion. Johnson told the people gathered at the meeting about the commissioners and about the surveyors from England. He said, "From their desire to make you all easy in your minds, they wou'd not go any further 'till they had obtained your voluntary Consent, and procured some of your People to be present, whom they wou'd pay for their attendance." He further said that to show their earnest truth in the matter, the commissioners had asked Johnson to lay before them a belt of wampum, which he did. A belt of wampum had even greater significance than strings. Belts were reserved for very important matters, such as matters concerning land. Johnson assured the council participants that the line being surveyed—the West Line—would not affect even the smallest bit of Indian land. Its purpose was only to settle a boundary-line dispute between the governors of Pennsylvania and Maryland. He showed them Governor Penn's letter. After further discussion, the council consented to the governors' request. They would select and send a group that would act as escorts for Mason and Dixon's crew.

On June 2, an express rider brought word of the Indians' consent to the surveyors at the Harlan home at the Brandywine. At last, Mason and Dixon could begin preparations to go west. They settled accounts with John Harlan and paid Joel Baily for repairing some instruments. On June 12, Jonathan Cope and six more instrument bearers departed for Fort Cumberland with the zenith sector; another wagon loaded with instruments soon followed. Last but not least, Mason and Dixon rehired Moses McClean, who in turn rehired many of the old crew. The surveyors also hired two guides. Unlike previous seasons, in which the surveyors had traveled across settled lands, surveying the far western line required the aid of men familiar with the area. Unpredictable rivers, steep cliffs, and boggy ground were only some of the obstacles that posed serious threats to the crew. Proceeding without guides would have been foolhardy. With the logistics well in hand, Mason and Dixon saddled up, this time for a journey into territory that was, as yet, largely unexplored by Europeans.

NATIVE AMBASSADORS

When Mason and Dixon arrived at Fort Cumberland on July 7, it bustled with a level of activity it hadn't seen in a while. There, the surveyors finally met Thomas Cresap. Knowing they would be living in tents for the next few months, they gladly accepted Cresap's invitation to spend the night at his beautiful estate near the fork of the Potomac River.

Meanwhile, Moses McClean finished final preparations. For this journey, the crew would need to haul more supplies than they had previously, when they were able to purchase provisions along the way. Wagons creaked under the weight of 657 pounds of bacon and 644 pounds of flour. Four bushels of oats for the packhorses shared a wagon bed with candles, thread, and ink powder. McClean even bought cooking pots for the Six Nations Indian escorts who would join them shortly. He employed more crewmen. Phinehas Davidson, whom they'd met the previous year while surveying near his home at mile 86, was one of the five cooks McClean hired. Like many of the crew hired during that summer and autumn, Davidson remained with the survey and worked full-time through mid-November.

The survey crew was a sight to behold as it chopped, jingled, and rumbled westward. At this point, the crew numbered more than sixty-five men, with eight instrument bearers, three tent keepers, and thirty-seven axmen among them. Trailing at the end of the party, fifty-five sheep, driven by shepherd James Reid, trotted along the newly blazed trail.

On July 16, just past mile 169, escorts from the Six Nations—fourteen Mohawks and Onondagas—arrived in camp accompanied by Hugh Crawford, their interpreter. Two of them, Soceena and Hannah, were women, the only women ever mentioned as traveling with the survey party.

Unbeknownst to Mason and Dixon, the boundary commissioners had narrowly avoided chaos for the survey party. In mid-June, the Pennsylvania commissioners had received word that 100 to 130 members of the Six Nations had assembled and were preparing to join the surveyors. Frantic about the enormous cost a group that large would add to the survey's already hefty budget (by December 1767, the survey's cost for the year would reach 6,600 pounds, three times the cost of the 1765 season) the commissioners took immediate action. They sent an express rider to deliver a message to another Indian agent, instructing him "to make the [Indians] a small present of powder and ball, flour and other necessaries as a satisfaction for their trouble" in assembling, and "to use his utmost endeavours to persuade them to return home." The commissioners stipulated that no more than one hundred pounds be used to purchase the presents.

Fully aware of frontier tensions, the commissioners cautioned Mason and Dixon:

As the public Peace and your own Security may greatly depend on the good Usage and kind Treatment of the Deputies [the Indian escorts], we commit them to your particular Care, and recommend it to you in the most earnest Manner not only to use them well yourselves but to be careful that they receive no Abuse or ill treatment from the Men you may employ in carrying on the said Work, and to do your utmost to protect them from, the Insults of all other persons whatsoever.

This admonishment was not only morally justified; it would also help keep the team safe.

DEATH STRIKES

For the next month, the crew and its Mohawk and Onandaga escorts pushed westward. Near the 189-mile mark, the group crossed General Braddock's road at the place where it swung north toward the site of Fort Duquesne. Familiar with the road's route, the crewmen knew they were approaching land traveled and used by members of the Lenni-Lenape and Shawnee tribes, traditional enemies of the Six Nations. At a snail's pace, growing more nervous with each step, the crew edged onward.

On August 17, at 199 miles 63 chains 68 links, tent keepers James Reid and Alexander and James McClean pitched camp. Not long afterward, thirteen Lenni-Lenape strode into camp. One of them — "the tallest man I ever saw," according to Mason — introduced himself as the nephew of a Lenni-Lenape named Captain Black-Jacobs. Hugh Crawford spoke with them and explained what the surveyors were doing. Mason did not mention how long the visitors stayed. But he and Dixon felt the visit went well, writing to commissioner Benjamin Chew, "We are all at present Brothers in a kind and friendly Manner." The visitors left the camp without

Sir

Since our last of the 25th of July we have continued the Line to the 199th Miles Post, from the Post marked West in Mr Bryan's Field: Here we set up the Sector and found we were 15 Chains to the North of the true Parallel: Here the Great Meadows, bears N W distant by Information about 6 or 7 Miles. ———

At 178 Miles the Little Meadows bore South distant about 2½ Miles ————

At 189 Miles 69 Chains we crosid General Bradocks Road on the Top of Winding Ridge. ————

At 194. 28 crosid the Yoahio Geni. ————

The Cheif (with one more) of the Mohoaks left us on Friday last, being desirous to return to their Country; having Bussiness (as they said) that required them at Home. ——— They chused to go by Harris's Ferry on Sasquehannah, on which directed them to the Care of Coll. Bird. ———

We have here recd a Visit from the Delawares 13 in No: and we are all at present Brothers in a kind and friendly Manner

We are Sr
Your most obedient and
humble Servants

The Line
About 10 Miles Easty
of Laurel Hill
25th Augst 1767

Cha: Mason

Jere Dixon

P.S.
We have here sent a sufficient No of Hands back to open a Visto in the true Parallel by the Time we shall finish another Station.

Mason and Dixon's 1767 letter to commissioner Benjamin Chew reporting the visit from the Lenni-Lenape, whom they referred to as Delawares further incident. Even so, the crew's unease grew. Perhaps the Mohawk and Onandaga escorts felt similarly, as on Friday, August 21, two of the Mohawks "left us . . . being desirous to return to their Country; having Business (as they said) that required them at Home."

Turning to their work, the surveyors divided the crew into two groups, one to clear the vista eastward, back toward Savage Mountain, the other to continue west. The men heading west worried that decreasing the number of their group could increase the likelihood of an attack by the Lenni-Lenape or the Shawnees.

In their free moments, Mason and Dixon swapped stories with Hugh Crawford. For nearly three decades, first as a trader and later as an officer in the French and Indian War, Crawford had traveled extensively in the lands west of the colonies. He'd visited the Ohio Territory and floated down the Mississippi River. He told the surveyors of wide rivers deep enough to accommodate large ships and sloops. He told them of rich, fertile land. He told them about Illinois, about eight hundred miles from where they were sitting, "through which you may travel 100 miles, and not find one Hill."

By September, the total number of the crew had swelled to more than 110. Even split into two groups, the traveling men, sheep, cows, horses, and the accompanying sounds of axes chopping wood created a noisy presence in the wilderness. The uneven, rough ground forced Moses McClean to replace wagons with packhorses. Thirty-two packhorse drivers tended as many as four or five horses each. Drivers William Baker and John Carpenter signed on at the end of August and quickly adjusted to the daily routine. When it was time to move camp, they roped food, barrels, kettles, and other supplies securely onto the horses' backs. At other times, Baker and Carpenter harnessed the horses and hauled felled trees and brush from the vista. Like all crewmen, they kept one ear cocked for warning shouts about falling trees so they could pull their horses out of harm's way.

GET A JOB!

*M*ASON AND DIXON *hired many men while they were in America. But they weren't the only employers looking for help. In colonial times, prospective employers placed want ads in the newspaper, just as they do today. Had you been looking for a job while the surveyors were hiring, here are some of the positions you would have seen advertised in the widely circulated* Pennsylvania Gazette:

WANTED, Able bodied *Negroe* Men and Boys, to work at a Brick yard, Likewise a Man that understands making and burning Pin and Pan Tiles, may have good Wages by applying to the Subscriber, in Race street, or at his Brick yard, near the Barracks.   *[March 22, 1764]*

WANTED, A person qualified to act as a Butler in a Gentleman Family. He must be able to write, and keep common Accounts; understand cleaning of Plate, &c. also dressing of Hair in the modern Taste.   *[August 9, 1764]*

WANTED . . . A young Girl, about 12 or 13 Years old, that can sew well, as an Apprentice to a genteel Business, with whom a handsome Fee will be expected.   *[September 9, 1765]*

WANTED, An Apprentice to a Watch maker; he must be a Lad of Genius, and of creditable Parents; he must serve Seven Years, and notwithstanding he will have an Opportunity (which is not very common in America) of making the Movement, and finishing the same, the Apprentice Fee (if small) provided the Boy suits, will be accepted.   *[November 20, 1766]*

WANTED, A family, that will undertake the care of a flock of sheep; for doing which they will have a good house (within three miles and a half of Philadelphia) part of an orchard, pasture for one cow, and a garden, rent free.   *[December 24, 1767]*

Fol: 13

1767

The Weekly Accompts of the Hands employed under ...
between Maryland & Pennsylvania with a ...
from the 7th Day of September to the ...

		Name	Role	Mon	Tue	Wed	Thu	Fri	Sat	Sun	
	1	Moses Barnes	Overseer of the Axemen a 5/0	1	1	1	1	1	6	1	
	2	Johnathan Cope	Chain Carrier a 3/0 p day	1	1	1	1	1	6	1	
	3	Samuel McClean	Ditto a Ditto	1	1	1	1	1	6	1	
	4	James McClean	Ditto a Ditto	1	1	1	1	1	6	1	
	5	Henry Matier	Ditto a Ditto	1	1	1	1	1	6	1	
	6	Robert Farlow	Instrument bearer a 5/	1	1	1	1	1	6	1	
	7	Robert Boggs	Ditto a Ditto	1	1	1	1	1	6	1	
	8	James Robison	Ditto a 5/0 p day	1	1	1	1	1	6	1	
	9	James Kain	Overseer of Axemen a 5/0 p day	1	1	1	1	1	6	1	
	10	William Farlow	Instrument bearer a 5/0 p day	1	1	1	1	1	6	2	
	11	Alexander McClean	Steward at Camp a 7/6 p day	1	1	1	1	1			
	12	John Reid	Tentkeeper a 4/0 p day	1	1	1	1	1	6	1	
	13	William Neely	Ditto a 4/0 p day	1	1	1	1	1	6	1	
	14	Andrew Thompson	Ditto a Ditto	1	1	1	1	1	6	1	
	15	Andrew Miller	Waggoner a 5/0 p day	1	1	1	1	1	6	1	
	16	Conrad Redheifer	Ditto a Ditto	1	1	1	1	1	6	1	
	17	Edward Coombes	Guide a 5/0 p day	1	1	1	1	1	6	1	
	18	Robert Bennet	Ditto a 5/0 p day	1	1	1	1	1	6	1	
	19	John Denny	Cook a 4/0 p day 7 days	1	1	1	1	1	1	1	
	20	Thomas Hynes	Ditto a Ditto	1	1	1	1	1	6	1	
	21	Hugh Campbel	Ditto a Ditto	1	1	1	1	1	6	1	
	22	John Nelson	Ditto a Ditto	1	1	1	1	1	6	1	
	23	Phineas Davidson	Ditto a Ditto	1	1	1	1	1	6	1	
	24	Samuel Miller	Ditto a Ditto	1	1	1	1	1	6	1	
	25	Edward Grimes	Ditto a Ditto	1	1	1	1	1	6	1	
	26	Robert Nelson	Axeman a 3/6 p day	1	1	1	1	1	6		
	27	James Steward	Ditto a Ditto	1	1	1	1	1	6	1	
	28	Joab Simms	Ditto a Ditto	1	1	1	1	1	6	1	
	29	Benjamin Speel	Ditto a Ditto	1	1	1	1	1	6	1	
	30	David Parks	Ditto a Ditto	1	1	1	1	1	6	1	
	31	Joseph Good	Ditto a Ditto	1	1	1	1	1	6	1	
	32	John Means	Ditto a Ditto	1	1	1	1	1	6	1	
	33	Jacob Kelly	Ditto a Ditto	1	1	1	1	1	6	1	
	34	Robert Smith	Ditto a Ditto	1	1	1	1	1	6	1	
	35	Felix Lar	Ditto a Ditto	1	1	1	1	1	6		
	36	David Cox Sr	Ditto a Ditto	1	1	1	1	1	6	1	
	37	Jonathan Cisney	Ditto a Ditto	1	1	1	1	1	6	1	
	38	James Blair	Ditto a Ditto	1	1	1	1	1	6	1	
	39	John Wood	Ditto a Ditto	1	1	1	1	1	6	1	
	40	Robert Boggs	Ditto a Ditto	1	1	1	1	1	6	1	
	41	Nicholas Miller	Ditto a Ditto	1	1	1	1	1	6	1	
	42	William Tyce	Ditto a Ditto	1	1	1	1	1	6	1	
	43	Richard Adams	Butcher a 3/6 p day	1	1	1	1	1	6	1	
	44	John Waters	Axeman a 3/6 p day	1	1	1	1	1	6	1	
	45	Joseph Barker	Ditto a Ditto	1	1	1	1	1	6	1	
	46	Solomon Corn	Ditto a Ditto	1	1	1	1	1	6	1	
	47	Nathan Linn	Ditto a Ditto	1	1	1	1	1	6	1	
	48	Lewis Rogers	Ditto a Ditto	1	1	1	1	1	6	1	
	49	Aron Huffam	Ditto a Ditto	1	1	1	1	1	6	1	
	50	Ovid McCrahon	Ditto a Ditto	1	1	1	1	1	6	1	
	51	Andrew Russel	Ditto a Ditto	1	1	1	1	1	6	1	
	52	Shedrick Foreman	Ditto a Ditto	1	1	1	1	1	6	1	
	53	Nathaniel McCarty	Ditto a Ditto	1	1	1	1	1	6	1	
	54	James Henthorn	Ditto a Ditto	1	1	1	1	1	6	1	
	55	Samuel Williamson	Ditto a Ditto	1	1	1	1	1	6	1	

Amount £

By September 7, 1767, Moses McClean needed two pages in his account book just to list the crew. Monies received were recorded on a separate, much shorter, page.

Mess.ʳˢ Mason & Dixon in running the West Line

Just Accompt of their Employment, Time & Wages
12 Day inclusive

1767

No.	Name	Occupation	Monday	Tuesday	Wednesday	Thursday	Friday	Saturday	Total	£	s	d
56	Samuel Gourley	Axman a 3/6 p day	1	1	1	1	6	1	1	0		
57	William Hinch	Do a Do	1	1	1	1	6	1	1	0		
58	John Mynan	Do a Do	1	1	1	1	6	1	1	0		
59	Laughlin McLean	Do a Do	1	1	1	1	6	1	1	0		
60	Evan Cifney	Do a Do	1	1	1	1	6	1	1	0		
61	Robert Means	Do a Do	1	1	1	1	6	1	1	0		
62	Robert McCleave	Do a Do	1	1	1	1	6	1	1	0		
63	John Gollogher Ser	Ditto a Do	1	1	1	1	6	1	1	0		
64	James Thomson	Ditto a Do	1	1	1	1	6	1	1	0		
65	Arthur Forbus	Ditto a Do	1	1	1	1	6	1	1	0		
66	James Gibson	Ditto a Do	1	1	1	1	6	1	1	0		
67	John Blair	Ditto a Do	1	1	1	1	6	1	1	0		
68	David Cox	Ditto a Ditto	1	1	1	1	6	1	1	0		
69	John Harper	Butcher a 3/6 p day	1	1	1	1	6	1	1	0		
70	James Reid	Shepher a 3/6 p day	1	1	1	1	6	1	1	0		
71	John Powel	Milk Maid a Do	1	1	1	1	6	1	1	0		
72	Thomas Hynes	Pack hors Driver a 3/6	1	1	1	1	6	1	1	0		
73	Andrew Hynes	Do a Do	1	1	1	1	6	1	1	8		
74	Jeremiah Stillwell	Do a Do	1	1	1	1	6	1	1			
75	Matthew Hamilton	Do a Do	1	1	1	1	6	1	1	0		
76	John Irwin	Do a Do	1	1	1	1	6	1	1	0		
77	William Stevenson	Do a Do	1	1	1	1	6	1	1	0		
78	Samuel Smith	Do a Do	1	1	1	1	6	1	1	0		
79	Alexander McDowel	Do a Do	1	1	1	1	6		4	0		
80	John Killogh	Do a Do	1	1	1	1	6		4	0		
81	Francis Killogh	Do a Do	1	1	1	1	6		4			
82	Robert Walt	Axman a 3/6 p day	1	1	1	1	6					
83	Ezekiel Killogh	Ditto a Do	1	1	1	1	6	1	1	0		
84	John Gollogher	Ditto a Do	1	1	1	1	6	1	1	0		
85	Will Cralsford	Ditto a Do	1	1	1	1	6	1	1	0		
86	Jacob Bainhart	Ditto a Do	1	1	1	1	6	1	1	0		
87	John McFeely	Ditto a Do	1	1	1	1	6	1	1	0		
88	James Bell	Ditto a Do	1	1	1	1	6	1	1	0		
89	Philip Richey	Ditto a Do	1	1	1	1	6	1	1	0		
90	William Downard	Ditto a Do	1	1	1	6		1	1	0		
91	Daniel Harris	Do a Do	0	0	0	0	6	1	1	0		
92	Thomas Abram	Do a Do	1	1	1	1	6	1	1	0		
93	Jehue Jonson	Do a Do	1	1	1	1	6	1	1	0		
94	William Baker	Do a Do	1	1	1	1	6	1	1	0		
95	John Carpenter	Do a Do	1	1	1	1	6	1	1	0		
96	Joseph Onlow	Do a Do	1	1	1	1	6	1	4	0		
97	William Bennet	Cook a 4/ Do	1	1	1	1	5	1	17	6		
98	William Spencer	Do a Do	1	1	1	1	5	1	4	0		
99	Jacob Downard	Do a Do	1	1	1	1	6	1	1	0		
100	John McGinnis	Do a Do	1	1	1	1	6	1	1	0		
101	James Stugale	Do a Do	1	1	1	1	6	1	7	0		
102	Samuel Bell	Pack Horseman a Do	1	1	1	1	6	1	7	0		
103	James McKinney	Axman a Do	1	1	1	1	6	1	7	0		
104	Samuel Howard	Do a Do	1	1	1	1	6	1	7	0		
105	William Marshel	Do a Do	1	1	1	1	6	1	7	0		
106	William Davidson	Do a Do	1	1	1	1	6	1	1	0		
107	David McMurey	Do a Do	1	1	1	1	6	1	1	0		
108	Henry Haglley	Do a Do	1	1	1	1	6	1	1	0		
109	Aron Henry	Do a Do	1	1	1	1	6	1	7	0		
110	Hugh Gilliland	Do a Do	1	1	1	1	6	1	1	0		
	Daniel Campbel	Store keeper at the Meadow	1	1	1	1	6	1				

Amount £

John Powel was in charge of different animals—cows! He is alternately listed in McClean's account ledger first as "Cow Milker" and thereafter as "Milk Maid." Due to lack of refrigeration, milk spoiled quickly. The only way the cooks could get fresh milk for cooking was by bringing cows with them. The herd eventually grew to ten.

When the crew paused along the banks of the Cheat River, Mason spent some time fishing. He was delighted when he "found plenty of fish of various sorts, and very large, particularly cat fish." Mason also caught a lizard nearly a foot long but made no mention of what he did with it. Dixon looked at the rocks in the area, easily identifying coal, which reminded him of his experiences in the coal mine his father operated.

While Mason and Dixon noticed fish and rocks, their Indian escorts wondered just how far west the surveyors planned to go. Mistrust of the crew's motives, as well as apprehension about encounters with enemy warriors, led to growing discontent. When two of the Mohawks heard that the surveyors intended to cross the Cheat River, they requested a meeting. Hugh Crawford and Mason and Dixon must have presented a convincing argument, because the escorts allowed the surveyors to cross the river and continue west.

Dr. Vause's medicines were useful for treatment of common ailments, but they were of no help on September 17. At 221 miles from the Post Marked West, Mason and Dixon sent instrument bearers to fetch the zenith sector from their previous camp. Camp setup was well under way. Packhorse drivers William Baker and John Carpenter were busy tending to their horses. And then an axman's blade bit into a tree trunk for one final blow. The tall tree leaned, slowly at first, and then faster as it toppled toward the ground. Unknowingly, Baker and Carpenter stood directly in its path. Before they could move, the heavy trunk crashed down. Both men died at once. News of the tragedy quickly spread through camp. That night, the deaths of William and John reminded everyone how dangerous their work was. Many of the men grumbled about their safety.

More visitors

On September 29, at the east bank of the Monongahela River, 222 miles from the Post Marked West, a group of twenty-six crewmen confronted Mason and Dixon. The visiting Lenni-Lenape had worried them, yet they had willingly stayed with the survey. However, crossing the Monongahela River meant that they were passing into Lenni-Lenape and Shawnee territory. Now they were afraid. And they could see that their Indian escorts were uneasy, too. The twenty-six men flatly refused to cross the river and announced that they were quitting. Nothing Mason or Dixon said changed their minds. The surveyors had no choice but to pay the men and release them. They did persuade the fifteen remaining axmen to stay and sent word to Forts Cumberland and Redstone for replacements for the twenty-six who'd quit, if they could be found. The remaining crew crossed the Monongahela, climbed its western bank, and walked deeper into Indian Territory.

Unbeknownst to Mason and Dixon, they were being watched. About two miles from the river, three Indians—two men and a woman—approached them. As the trio was dressed almost completely in European-style clothing, the surveyors had no idea to which tribe they might belong. But the Mohawks immediately recognized them as Lenni-Lenape. Stepping forward, the leader of the Mohawk escorts greeted the visitors. He learned that the older man was Catfish, a "Chief of the Delaware Nation." Catfish's wife and nephew accompanied him. As custom required, the men sat and held a council, during which the Mohawk leader presented Catfish with two strings of wampum. He then explained who Mason and Dixon were, what they were doing, and why members of the Six Nations were with them. Catfish accepted the wampum and promised to bring it to the people of his town and relay what he had been told. Though the meeting was cordial, even the Mohawks and Onondagas were disquieted after Catfish left.

New workers from Fort Cumberland arrived at the end of the first week in October. Almost on their heels, a party of eight Senecas arrived. The Indian escorts welcomed them gladly, since the Senecas were members of the Six Nations. The Seneca party, equipped "with Blankets and Kettles, Tomahawks Guns and Bows and Arrows," was on its way south to fight the Cherokee. They decided to travel with the survey party for a time. During that time, all of the Indians and Hugh Crawford discussed news from distant council fires. The Lenni-Lenape and Shawnees weren't the only angry Indian groups; the Six Nations peoples also felt a growing mistrust toward European colonists. After two days, the surveyors gave the Senecas some gunpowder and war paint, and the party resumed its journey south. Yet the Indian escorts who still remained with the survey continued discussing matters among themselves.

On October 9, 1767, at 231 miles 20 chains, the surveyors crossed a well-trodden Indian warpath. Within two miles, the chief of the Mohawks requested a meeting with Mason and Dixon. "This day the Chief of the Indians which joined us on the 16th of July informed us that the above mentioned War Path was the extent of his commission from the Chiefs of the Six Nations that he should go with us, with the Line; and that he would not proceed one step farther Westward." For a day, Mason and Dixon pled their case to continue west: they had almost reached Pennsylvania's western limit—five degrees of longitude from the Delaware River. But the escorts would not budge, and the surveyors had no choice but to accept their decision. William Johnson later informed Richard Peters that the Mohawk leader had "Suppressed part of what

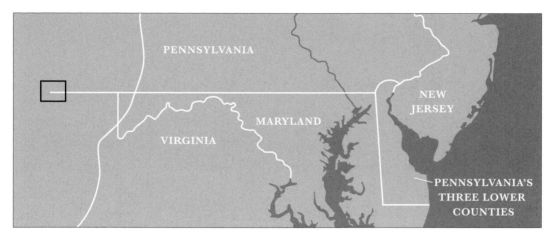

The black rectangle inset marks the end point of the West Line.

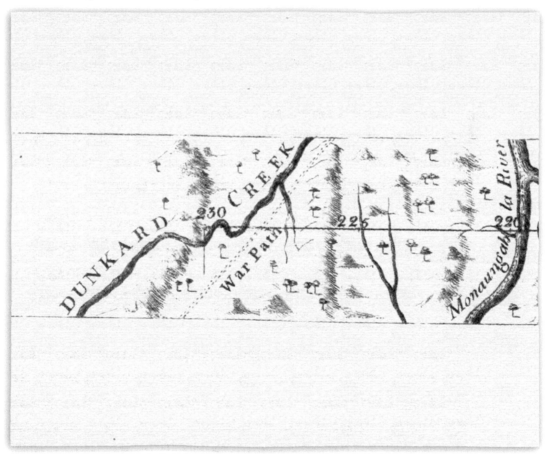

On his final map, Dixon even included the Indian War Path that Mason noted in his journal.

he might have informed you." Suspicions of English deceit, grievances over broken promises, and rumors of Indian enslavement — circulated by French agitators — had pushed the Indians to a level of anger higher than Johnson had ever seen, short of war. Although it arrived after the fact, this information further validated Mason and Dixon's acceptance of the escorts' decision.

Near a ridge now called Browns Hill, Mason and Dixon established their westernmost camp and spent the week of October 11 observing the stars. While they were there, a large group of Lenni-Lenape, among them Prisqueetom, brother to the king of the Lenni-Lenape, visited the camp. Prisqueetom, who was eighty-six years old, told Mason that he and his brother "had a great mind to go and see the great King over the Water; and make a perpetual Peace with him; but was afraid he should not be sent back to his own Country."

In this western camp, the surveyors monitored their five key stars — Vega, Deneb, Sadr, Delta Cygni, and Capella — for the last time. These stars, old friends by then, had guided them along the West Line for more than a year. And it was time for another marker:

> On the top of a very lofty Ridge . . . at the distance of 233 miles 17 Chains 48 Links from the Post marked West in Mr. Bryan's Field, we set up a Post marked W on the West Side and heaped around it Earth and Stone three yards and a half diameter at the Bottom, and five feet High.

With cutting-edge scientific instrumentation, meticulous observation, and a hardworking crew, Mason and Dixon had successfully broken the established boundaries of what a survey could accomplish. Even though the West Line ended short of Pennsylvania's western limit, Mason and Dixon's very, very long West Line still inscribed a parallel of latitude on Earth's surface — the first of its kind anywhere.

THE END OF THE LINE

Although the West Line survey was complete, a lot of work remained. As soon as the team erected the stone cairn, axmen began cutting the vista east to milepost 199, where it would connect with an already completed section of the vista. Tensions eased as the group returned to familiar territory.

Sadly, though, another death occurred. Jacob, one of the Indian escorts who had worked many years as a scout for the British, died of an unmentioned cause. The surveyors had a coffin made for him and purchased a black burial shroud. Jacob's remains, along with "a silk handkerchief sent to his widow," were carried to Philadelphia, where he was "decently buried." Jacob's pay of forty dollars, a higher amount than that paid to most of the other Indians, was sent to his widow.

On November 5, Hugh Crawford and the Indians departed. They were paid, in colonial currency, a total of 631 dollars (the equivalent of slightly more than 236 pounds) for their service. The Mohawk Leaders—Hendricks, Daniel, and Peter—received payment twice that of the other escorts. Three of the men also received a rifle in partial payment. Soceena and Hannah received payment equal to that of the lower-paid Indian men. Shortly after the Indians left, all but thirteen of the survey's crewmen departed for their homes too.

Meanwhile, the final load of boundary stones lay waiting at the foot of Sideling Hill, at milepost 134. Earlier that season, Mason and Dixon had received an estimate for transporting them to the section of the line between mileposts 134 and 199. The exorbitant fee requested was twelve pounds—nearly equal to the weekly wages of a dozen crewmen! Astounded, Mason and Dixon refused, a decision later applauded by Pennsylvania commissioner Benjamin Chew, who complimented the surveyors, noting they had "acted very prudently in refusing to give the extravagant Price." Mason sent a letter to Hugh Hamersley, Lord Baltimore's agent, to report that they'd left seventy boundary stones at Fort Frederick. Ironically, considering the expense of cutting the stones and shipping them to America, Mason wrote, "In all the Mountains we have past over this year and almost at every Mile Post there is good stone if not superior to those sent from England." In lieu of the heavy markers, Mason and Dixon followed the commissioners' instructions and, without any further visits from the Lenni-Lenape, marked the line on the tops of the western ridges with cairns similar to the one on the westernmost ridge. The work satisfied them: "The Marks we have erected may be seen from Ridge to Ridge in most Places and it will take a great length of Time (if ever) to destroy them."

The crew marched east in snowy weather that grew progressively worse. At Savage Mountain, they trudged through snow twelve to fourteen inches deep. On November 20, with hands so cold their fingers wouldn't open and close, they sheltered in a Mr. Kellam's house, where seven of the crewmen quit. Cold, tired, and forced to find new men to complete the work, Mason and Dixon splurged on a filling, hot meal. On November 28, after paying the crewmen, the surveyors sat down to a hearty dinner of venison, corn pudding, and turnips.

Later, when the surveyors reached the top of Town Hill, they received a pleasant surprise: Robert Farlow, a trusted instrument bearer who'd worked with them for three years, awaited them. In the beginning of October, Mason and Dixon had sent him east to set boundary stones on an eastern section of the line. When the surveyors arrived on Town Hill, Farlow and his men had just finished building the cairn there. Mason and Dixon were even more pleased when Farlow told them all the markers were in place from milepost 135 eastward to the Post marked West, except for those at miles 77 and 117, which they'd placed slightly off the line due to marshy ground and a gigantic boulder. As the size of the crew dwindled, Moses McClean began selling off unneeded equipment: blankets, kettles, two axes, a pair of hobbles, a saddle, a tent, and ten cows.

By December 12, a skeleton crew of fewer than ten men remained with Mason and Dixon, who dispatched an express message to the commissioners to expect their arrival in Philadelphia—mission accomplished—on the fifteenth of December.

The surveyors spent Christmas Day meeting with the commissioners, including Benjamin Chew, who was eager "to put an end to this tedious Business." Mason and Dixon were relieved to hear the commission had "no further occasion for us to run any more Lines for the Honorable Proprietors." Was their work for the Penns and Lord Baltimore finally done?

Not quite yet

It seemed not, as almost in its next breath, the boundary commission issued two additional tasks. First, Dixon, a fine draftsman, was to draw a map of the line. Second, knowing that Mason and Dixon were computing the length of a degree of latitude for the Royal Society, the commissioners asked them to compute the length of a degree of longitude in the parallel of the West Line. The surveyors undertook both tasks at the Harlans' house.

The second task took a week of mathematical computation. Using their many star observations and chain measurements, and supposing Earth was a perfect sphere, Mason and Dixon calculated the length of a degree of longitude along the West Line to be 53.5549 miles. However, in their note to Richard Peters, Mason wrote, "But the Earth is not known to be exactly a Spheroid, nor whether it is everywhere of equal Density. . . . We do not give in this as accurate." One task was complete.

Dixon finished drawing the map at the end of January, and they delivered it to Mr. Peters for his approval on January 29. While in Philadelphia, they stopped at the State House and checked on the zenith sector and transit instruments, confirming that they were still safely stored. With the second task completed, they decided to finish computing a degree of latitude for the Royal Society.

On February 1, Mason and Dixon prepared to gather the rest of the information they needed to measure and compute a degree of latitude. Joined by their good friend Joel Baily and a few others, Mason and Dixon laboriously remeasured the distance from the Harlans' garden all the way to the Middle Point. Even though they had already measured the distance in 1764 with a Gunter's chain, the Royal Society wanted more precision. They wanted the distance measured with four brass-tipped wooden rods, each ten feet long, and a five-foot-long brass standard, all sent directly to Mason and Dixon for this purpose by Nevil Maskelyne. Maskelyne especially cautioned Mason and Dixon to "Keep the rods as dry as you can, for if any thing alters their length it is to be supposed to be changes of moisture and dryness. . . . Always take care to bring the ends of the rods to meet, without any shock, and don't trust this to your Labourers." Maskelyne didn't trust anyone but Mason and Dixon. Every measurement was double-checked.

They recorded the temperature multiple times during the day. Their reason for doing so was that in addition to the wet and dry changes mentioned by Maskelyne, changes in temperature slightly altered the length of the wooden rods, the wood expanding in heat and shrinking in cold.

The trip to the Middle Point lasted from February 23 until June 4. Wading through swampy water became routine. Twice they crossed water that was four to five feet deep. Both times, Mason noted that it was others, not he, who went in that water.

At the Middle Point, they lodged for several days at Mr. Twiford's house, one of Mason's favorite places in America, before returning to the Harlans' house, where Mason combined the earlier data collected at the Middle Point with the crew's new measurements. He calculated that the length of a degree of latitude—the arc of the meridian from the Stargazer's Stone to the Middle Point—at their location was equal to 68.81 miles—a 0.69-mile difference from the measurement of a degree of latitude in Europe. While the difference might seem small, it did help scientists prove that Earth was not perfectly spheroidal—an important confirmation. Mason submitted the results to the Royal Society, which received the information with great appreciation.

The Royal Society was delighted that Mason and Dixon had successfully measured a degree of latitude in North America. The vertical line at the center of the map is the degree that they measured.

It was nearly the end of June before the surveyors completed their measurements and calculations. As soon as they finished, they notified the boundary-line commissioners that they were ready to leave for England. Rather than agreeing, the commissioners instead informed the surveyors that they wanted Dixon's map engraved and printed before the two men departed. One of the commissioners hired Mr. Dawkins, a local engraver, to do the work. Unfortunately, Dawkins quit midway through the job. Engraver James Smither completed the work, and the copper plate was delivered to Robert Kennedy's printing office on Third Street in Philadelphia. Mason and Dixon stepped closer to their departure for home when they picked up two hundred copies of the boundary-line map on August 16. Mr. Smither presented his bill for engraving several days later. It was for twelve pounds—the exact amount Mason

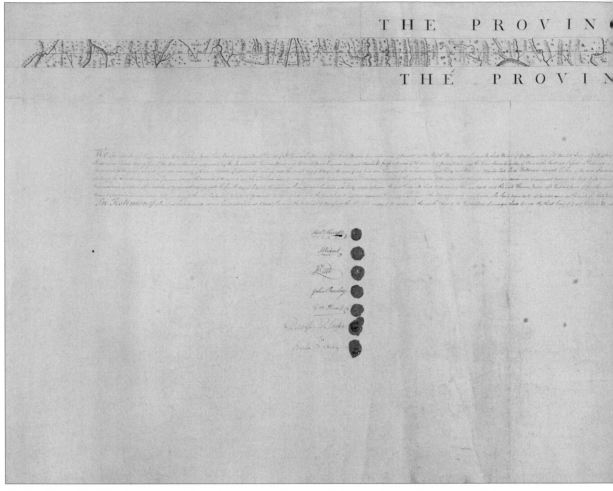

Copies of Jeremiah Dixon's map were delivered to the boundary commissioners, who signed and stamped their acceptance of the map with wax seals. The column on the left contains the Maryland commissioners' signatures; the column on the right has those of the commissioners from Pennsylvania.

and Dixon had saved by not hauling boundary stones to the tops of the farthest western ridges.

Mason and Dixon spent the next three weeks settling their accounts, wrapping up loose ends, and attending one final meeting with the commissioners. On September 8, almost five years after they had arrived in America, Charles Mason and Jeremiah Dixon said good-bye to Philadelphia and journeyed to New York. On September 11, 1768, at 11:30 in the morning, they boarded the *Halifax Packet* and set sail for

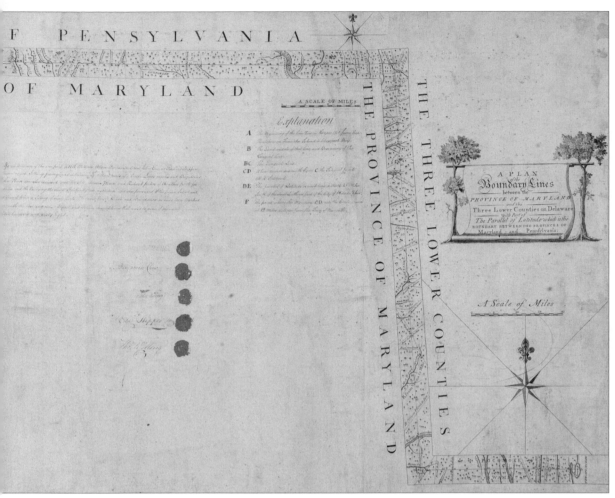

Maryland commissioners: Horatio Sharpe, John Ridout, John Leeds, John Barclay, George Stewart, Daniel of St. Thomas Jenifer, and John Beale Bordley. Pennsylvania commissioners: William Allen, Benjamin Chew, John Ewing, Edward Shippen Jr., and Thomas Willing.

Falmouth, England. The same day, Mason concluded his journal, writing, "Thus ends my restless progress in America."

For most of the colonists, Mason and Dixon's line resolved the territorial disputes that had pitted landowners against each other. But a few colonists, especially those whose lands straddled the line, battled on, filing land disputes that had to be decided in court. Sometimes the result was that a colonist from one province lost his property to a claimant from the other province. These out-of-luck colonists had no choice but to move.

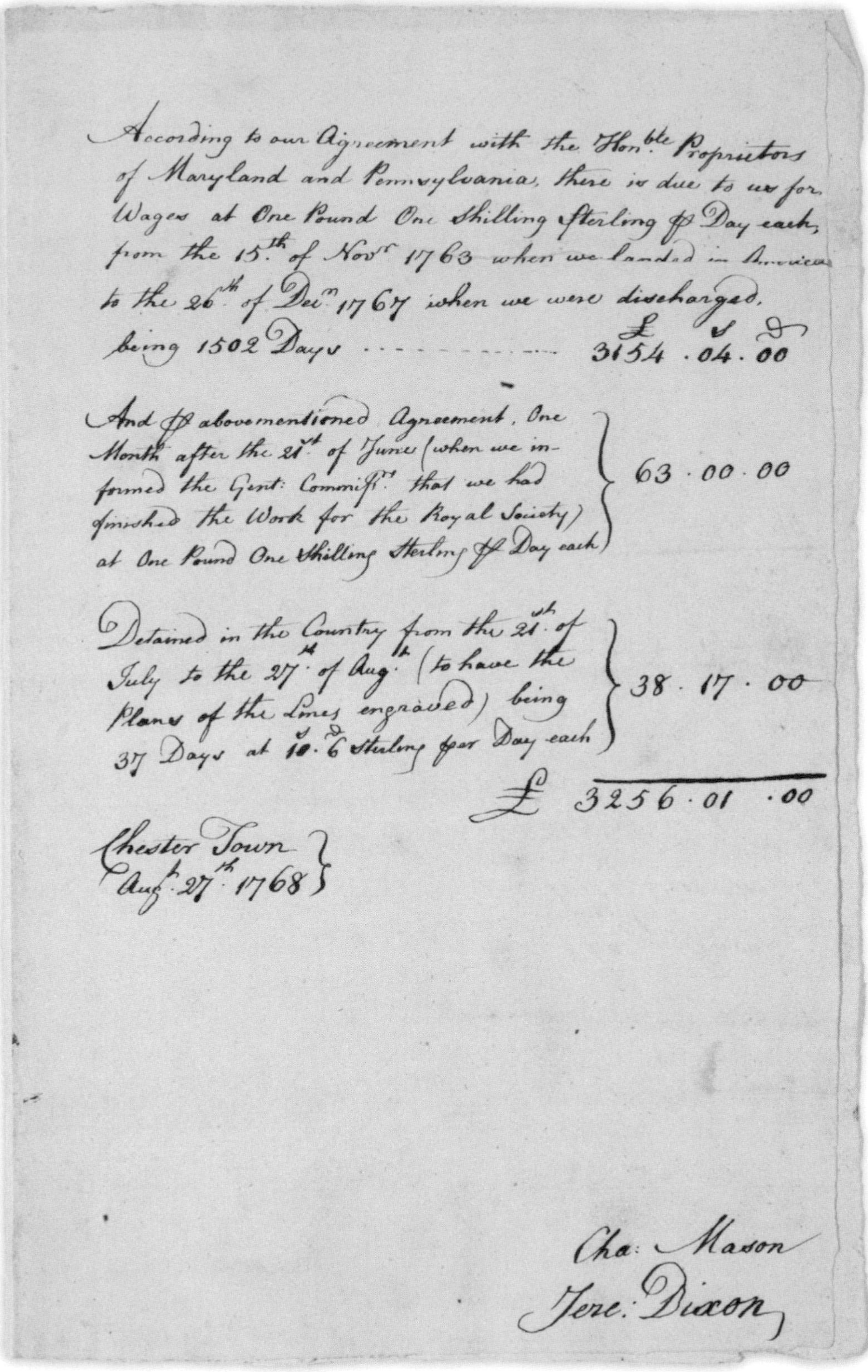

According to our Agreement with the Hon.ble Proprietors of Maryland and Pennsylvania, there is due to us for Wages at One Pound One Shilling Sterling ⅌ Day each, from the 15.th of Nov.r 1763 when we landed in America to the 26.th of Dec.m 1767 when we were discharged, being 1502 Days ----------------

£ 3154 . 04 . 00

And ⅌ abovementioned Agreement, One Month after the 21.st of June (when we informed the Gent: Commiss.rs that we had finished the Work for the Royal Society) at One Pound One Shilling Sterling ⅌ Day each

63 . 00 . 00

Detained in the Country from the 21.st of July to the 27.th of Aug.t (to have the Plans of the Lines engraved) being 37 Days at 10.s 6.d Sterling ⅌ Day each

38 . 17 . 00

£ 3256 . 01 . 00

Chester Town
Aug.t 27.th 1768

Cha: Mason
Jere: Dixon

In August 1768, shortly before they left Pennsylvania, Mason and Dixon gave Benjamin Chew their invoice for 1,502 days' worth of work. The total bill was for 3,256 pounds, one shilling.

Chapter ✴ *Twelve*

FREEDOM'S BOUNDARY

MASON AND DIXON'S survey was done. Eight years later, the Declaration of Independence essentially made the Calvert and Penn boundary dispute moot. Under an agreement called the Articles of Confederation, the thirteen American colonies, among them Pennsylvania, Maryland, and Delaware, bound themselves (as sovereign states) into the United States of America in a combined fight against England. Proprietorships granted by England no longer applied. In 1776, concerned about one of the new nation's boundaries—the one between Virginia (West Virginia did not become a state until 1863) and Pennsylvania—Thomas Jefferson wrote to fellow Virginian and politician Edmund Pendleton, stating, "I wish they would compromise by an extension of Mason & Dixon's line. They do not agree to the temporary line proposed by our [Virginia] assembly."

After the Revolutionary War, Mason and Dixon's line remained the boundary separating the three states, although minor disputes continued over a small wedge of land where the three states converged. During the years 1782 to 1785, several surveyors completed the West Line by extending it to five degrees longitude, bringing the total length of the line to about 260 miles. People of the time were well aware of Mason and Dixon's line; it became part of everyday language. In 1784, a letter excerpted in the July 7 issue of the newspaper *Freeman's Journal* described the approach of a severe storm: "The storm then took across the ridge and made as clear a line as ever Mason and Dixon did."

During the early decades of the nineteenth century, perceptions of the origin of the Mason-Dixon Line had already blurred. In fact, in the 1830s, a number of newspapers printed short articles that reminded readers of the line's roots in a dispute between two feuding colonies. They did so because Mason and Dixon's line had begun to act as a boundary not just between states but between two new identities, and these new perceptions altered the lives of millions of Americans.

As tensions increased between northern and southern states, particularly issues concerning taxation of goods, people increasingly regarded Mason and Dixon's line as the division between the North and the South—not only geographically but also politically. For the most part, industry and manufacturing drove the North economically. Political decisions supported growth in those areas. In contrast, agriculture, particularly the cotton crop, drove the southern economy. Shipping cotton to overseas markets was big business. Political decisions favored increased crop production, which required increased labor—labor most often supplied by slaves. Slavery, at first on economic grounds, later on moral grounds, became a hotly debated issue as the United States expanded into new territories in the West. Tensions between the North and South escalated. In the June 24, 1833, issue of the *Connecticut Courant*, a man recalled a conversation he had had with the late John Randolph, a congressman and senator from Roanoke, Virginia. Randolph had been sending books to England for binding. When asked why he didn't use binderies in New York or Philadelphia, he had replied, "What Sir, patronize our Yankee task-masters who have imposed such a duty upon foreign books! Never, Sir, never! I will neither wear what they make, nor eat what they raise . . . and until I can have my books properly bound *south* of 'Mason and Dixon's line,' I shall employ John Bull" (meaning England). On October 9, 1841, Terre Haute's *Wabash Courier* editorialized, "This famous line is so often mentioned in and out of Congress that to American ears its name is familiar as household words."

At the same time, Mason and Dixon's line came to symbolize the boundary between freedom and slavery. This perception of the line may have started when Pennsylvania passed a new law in 1780.

A FREEDOM LINE

On March 1, 1780, the Pennsylvania legislature passed the Act for the Gradual Abolition of Slavery. While it did not set free the many slaves living in the state, it started the process. First, the law required slaveholders to register their slaves with government authorities by November 1, 1780; unregistered slaves would be considered free. The law was not unanimously popular. Slaveholder George Stevenson, who lived in Carlisle, resentfully complied. On October 7, he registered his three male slaves, Dick, Phil, and Mills. On the register, he wrote a comment stating he did so "in obedience to an useless Act of the General Assembly of the Common-Wealth of Pennsylvania, entitled 'An Act for the Gradual Abolition of Slavery.'"

Second, the act declared that a child born of a mother who was a slave would become free when she or he turned twenty-eight years old.

Taking advantage of loopholes in the law, some slaveholders avoided freeing younger slaves by selling them out of state before they reached that age or by sending a pregnant woman to another state, where the baby would be born under the slave laws applicable there. In 1788, to stop these evasions of the law, an act was passed that required the birth of an African-American child to be registered with the state government; it also prohibited sending enslaved pregnant women out of state.

At the same time, Quakers who supported abolition on moral and ethical grounds increasingly pressured Quakers who owned slaves to free them. Gradually, they responded. Together, the abolition act and the slaveholders who manumitted their slaves made a huge difference. Between 1780 and 1782, 6,855 slaves lived in Pennsylvania; in 1810, that number had been reduced to 795.

When the Pennsylvania assembly passed the 1780 abolition act, Mason and Dixon's West Line literally became a boundary line between a free state and a slave state. But the Mason-Dixon Line between Maryland and Delaware — the Tangent Line — was not. Both Maryland and Delaware were slave states. And not all of the states north of Mason and Dixon's line were free states, either. New York did not begin gradual abolition until 1799; New Jersey began gradual abolition in 1804. (Both states stipulated that children born of mothers who were slaves would be free, but only after serving as indentured servants into their twenties.)

The issue of slave states versus free states persisted as the United States expanded its boundary farther west. Ohio (1803), Indiana (1816), and Illinois (1818) were admitted into the union as free states. The Ohio River was and is the southern border of these states. As such, it was a boundary line between these three free states and the slave states of Kentucky and Virginia. (Perhaps because people had come to perceive Mason and Dixon's line as the boundary between slave and free states, they thought the Ohio River boundary was an extension of the line. But the two surveyors never worked farther west than Browns Hill.) Louisiana (1812), Mississippi (1817), and Alabama (1819) were admitted to the Union as slave states. A huge controversy arose when Missouri petitioned for statehood, because its status would upset the balance of slave and free states, which in 1819 stood at eleven states each. Balance was maintained through the Missouri Compromise, which was enacted in 1820. It allowed Missouri (1821) to enter the union as a slave state and Maine (1820) to do so as a free state. According to the Missouri Compromise, slavery was banned in the vast Louisiana Territory from latitude 36°30' N, with the exception of the land used to create the state of Missouri. All of the Louisiana Territory was more than 500 miles west of the end of Mason and Dixon's line. Yet people incorrectly associate the Missouri Compromise with their line.

RUN!

In 1849, Edward Gorsuch lived near Glencoe, in Baltimore County, Maryland, less than twenty miles south of milepost 44 along the West Line. The Gorsuch family roots ran deep; they'd lived in Maryland since the mid-seventeenth century. Edward Gorsuch had a wife and family. Friends and neighbors reported him to be a dignified, well-mannered man who taught Bible class at the Methodist church. He had inherited his farm of several hundred acres from his uncle, and he cared for it well, growing wheat and corn. He owned cows, sheep, pigs, and chickens. He also owned twelve slaves, a high number considering that only 10 percent of Maryland's slaveholders owned eight or more slaves. To Gorsuch, everything on the farm—the land, the animals, the slaves—was his property.

In 1849, more free blacks, about 74,700, lived in Maryland than in any other state. But Maryland had an even larger population of slaves, about 90,300. Between June 1849 and June 1850, 279 slaves escaped from Maryland. Four of them—Noah Buley, Nelson Ford, George Hammond, and Joshua Hammond (whose ages ranged from nineteen to the mid-twenties)—ran away from Edward Gorsuch.

THE FUGITIVE SLAVE ACT OF 1850

THE FUGITIVE SLAVE ACT OF 1850 was not the first law concerning escaped slaves. Fifty-seven years earlier, the Fugitive Slave Act of 1793 had required the return of runaway slaves. In the years since then, the issue of whether or not to require the return of escaped slaves had raged even more fiercely between abolitionists and slaveholders. Many abolitionists in northern states where slavery had been abolished completely ignored the 1793 law on the grounds that slavery was not permitted in their state. Southern slave owners demanded a law that would force free states to return their fugitive slaves. The Compromise of 1850 addressed slavery in the West and banned slavery in Washington, D.C. It also included the Fugitive Slave Act of 1850, which strengthened the earlier act.

Among its many mandates, the new act required that government marshals—even those in free states—"obey and execute all warrants . . . issued under the provisions of this act." A fine of one thousand dollars was issued if the official refused. Slave owners could obtain a warrant for the slave's arrest, pursue him or her into the free state or territory to which he or she had fled, and apprehend him or her. The slave owner could also hire an agent to act on his or her behalf. Any person who obstructed or hindered a slave owner, his agent, or any other person lawfully assisting him or her would be fined up to a thousand dollars and be sentenced to up to six months in prison. Furthermore, "In no trial or hearing under this act shall the testimony of such alleged fugitive be admitted in evidence . . . and [the warrant] shall be conclusive of the right of [the slave owner or agent] to remove such fugitive to the State or Territory from which he escaped." The act drew very specific legal boundaries that outlined the rights of the slaveholder. The fugitive slave was given no rights at all.

The four fugitives' freedom journey started with wheat. After the autumn harvest was stored, Gorsuch discovered that some of the grain was missing. A Quaker miller told Gorsuch that Abraham Johnson, a free black man who lived nearby, had offered to sell him a number of bushels of wheat. The miller said Johnson had gotten the wheat from four of Gorsuch's slaves. Gorsuch obtained a state warrant for Abraham Johnson's arrest. Hearing this, Johnson hid, and later fled north. Meanwhile, the slaves planned their escape. The night of November 6, 1849, the four men, aided by another of Gorsuch's slaves, made their way north. They crossed the Mason-Dixon Line into Pennsylvania.

Gorsuch could not comprehend why his slaves had left; he felt he had treated them well, and they knew they would be freed at age twenty-eight. He concluded that they had been led astray, and he believed they would return to his farm if given the choice. For nearly two years, Gorsuch followed the rumor trail in the hope of discovering their where-abouts. Finally, in August 1851, he received creditable word from one of his agents, a man named William Padgett, that the men were liv-ing in Lancaster County, Pennsylvania, near the town of Christiana. At that time, a group of white men called the Gap Gang spied on black people in the area in an attempt to find people who fit the description of fugitive slaves. They alerted slave owners. They terrorized the black community. And they even kidnapped black men and women — making no distinction between a free person of color or a fugitive slave — and took them across the boundary line into Maryland. They justified their actions as upholding the Fugitive Slave Act. Many locals believed that Padgett belonged to the Gap Gang.

Gorsuch assembled an armed posse that included his son Dickinson, a cousin, a nephew, and two neighbors. On September 9, in Philadelphia, under the auspices of the Fugitive Slave Act, he obtained four arrest warrants for his escaped slaves. He arranged to rendezvous with U.S. deputy marshal Henry Kline near Christiana. Two policemen Gorsuch had hired to accompany the posse never showed up.

RIOT!

Before dawn on September 11, 1851, a disguised guide led the posse, who traveled on foot so as not to alert the fugitives, to a road leading to a stone house occupied by tenant farmers William Parker; his wife, Eliza (both of whom had been fugitive slaves); and his in-laws, Alexander and Hannah Pinckney. Gorsuch's informant had reported that two of his fugitive slaves, living under the assumed names Joshua Kite and Samuel Thompson, were hiding inside Parker's house. Gorsuch reckoned he would soon have his slaves back under his control. He didn't

William Parker and the other African Americans barricaded on the second floor of his home refused to be intimidated by Edward Gorsuch and Deputy Kline. An argument between Gorsuch and one of the fugitives escalated into a riot.

know that an informer in the black community saw the posse traveling on the road the previous night and had alerted Parker, a fierce freedom fighter. And he was unaware that freeman Abraham Johnson, the man who had tried to sell Gorsuch's wheat back in Maryland, was also inside Parker's house.

Parker later stated that as the posse neared the house, it encountered Joshua Kite, who had gone outside. When Kite fled back inside, Kline and Gorsuch followed him in and climbed halfway up the staircase to the second floor.

Parker met them on the landing and told Deputy Kline he would not surrender. Gorsuch, at the bottom of the stairs, told Kline that the law was on his side. Kline agreed and stated that he could arrest the people in Parker's house. After a short time, someone in Parker's group threw a fish gig (a pronged instrument used to hook fish) down the stairs, followed by an ax. More discussion followed. According to Parker, Gorsuch said to him, "You have my property," to which Parker replied, "Go in the room down there, and see if there is anything there belonging to you. There are beds and a bureau, chairs, and other things. Then go out to the barn; there you will find a cow and some hogs. See if any of them are yours." Gorsuch said, "They are not mine; I want my men. They are here, and I am bound to have them." The two men held opposite viewpoints: Parker was defending people and their right to freedom; Gorsuch sought to reclaim property.

Sunrise approached. Heated conversation continued. Gorsuch insisted. Parker refused. Deputy Kline hemmed, hawed, and threatened to "set the house on fire, and burn them up." At that point, Mrs. Parker grabbed a horn used as a signal for help by the black community in a time of trouble. She went to the window and blew it long and loud. A few minutes later, she repeated the call. The horn's blare brought on a hail of gunfire from the posse. Shouts and calls for further discussion led to a fifteen-minute truce, followed by more talk between Parker and Gorsuch. Parker later claimed that Gorsuch was carrying two pistols; Dickinson Gorsuch said his father was unarmed.

Meanwhile, Castner Hanway and another of Parker's white neighbors, believing the posse to be kidnappers, hurried to Parker's house. Both men were well aware the Gap Gang kidnapped African Americans. Hanway asked to see the deputy's warrants. Even as Hanway read the warrants, members of the black community armed with guns, clubs, corn cutters, and scythes arrived in response to Mrs. Parker's signal. Later reports as to how many people arrived vary widely, ranging from fifteen to three hundred. Based on the 1850 U.S. census for the number of black people living in the area, a reasonable estimate is about twenty-five.

By the time these men assembled in the orchard in front of Parker's house, tempers had reached the boiling point. Kline urged the posse to back off; Hanway urged Deputy Kline to leave. The crowd pressed forward. Kline leaped the fence and disappeared into the grain field, but Edward Gorsuch stood resolute. Fugitive Samuel Thompson went outside and argued with Gorsuch. Then he seized Alexander Pinckney's rifle and clubbed Gorsuch. When Gorsuch rose, Thompson hit him again. And then the shooting started. No one knows who shot first. Chaos reigned. People screamed, shouted, and ran.

The whole confrontation, from first words through the riot that followed, lasted two hours. At the end of that time, Edward Gorsuch — shot, stabbed, and beaten — lay dead in Parker's front yard. His son Dickinson, seriously wounded by a shotgun blast to his side, lay in the field. Two bullets fired by Dickinson had passed through Parker's hat and sheared off some hair but had not drawn blood. Two other members of Parker's party were wounded: one in the hand, the other in the thigh. Gorsuch's nephew was severely beaten. Quaker Levi Pownall, who owned the Parkers' house, arrived at the scene and asked Parker for a blanket to cover Edward Gorsuch's body and for some water to give Dickinson. Parker told him to take anything he needed. Afterward, Pownall took Dickinson to his house. Contrary to everyone's prediction, Dickinson recovered, although it took many weeks. Edward Gorsuch's body was shipped by train to his family in Maryland.

Advised by friends to leave Pennsylvania, William Parker, his brother-in-law Alexander Pinckney, and Abraham Johnson traveled a circuitous four-hundred-mile journey by foot, wagon, and stage to Rochester, New York, where they stayed in the home of well-known abolitionist and former slave Frederick Douglass. He made arrangements for their safe passage by steamer out of the United States into Canada. By September 21, Parker and the others were safely in Kingston, Ontario.

Three years before the riot, Frederick Douglass, pictured here, said, "I have stood on each side of Mason and Dixon's line; I have endured the frightful horrors of slavery, and have enjoyed the blessings of freedom."

In an editorial in his newspaper, *Frederick Douglass' Paper*, on September 25, 1851, Douglass addressed the question of Parker's group and their right to step across the boundary line between slavery and freedom, as well as the boundary line between the law and moral right:

> If it be right for any man to resist those who would enslave them, it was right for the men of color at Christiana to resist. . . . For never were there, never can there be more sacred rights to defend than were menaced on this occasion. Life and liberty are the most sacred of all man's rights.

Douglass escorted Parker, Johnson, and Pinckney to the wharf the day they left for Canada. Remaining with them until the gangplank was being hauled in, Douglass received a last-minute "gift" from Parker: "I shook hands with my friends, received from Parker the revolver that fell from the hand of Gorsuch when he died, presented now as a token of gratitude and a memento of the battle for Liberty at Christiana." He further added that "this affair, at Christiana, . . . inflicted fatal wounds on the fugitive slave bill."

Meanwhile, in Christiana, thirty-eight people had been imprisoned in the riot's aftermath. Many of the black men were arrested with no evidence other than Deputy Kline's declaration that he recognized them as having been present. A few of his accusations were later proven untrue. On November 24, 1851, the trial of Castner Hanway, the neighbor who urged Kline to leave Parker's house, began. He was charged with treason against the United States. If he was convicted, the penalty would be death.

For eighteen days, in a courtroom with standing room only, the judge and jury listened as witnesses testified about Hanway's words and actions on September 11. Before the jury began its deliberations, the judge spoke to its members. He told them they had the right to make their own decision, but that, having heard the facts of the case, he felt bound to offer his opinion, which the jury could take into account or not, as they chose. He said he did not believe there was any proof "of previous conspiracy to make a *general* and *public resistance to any law* of the United States." He further noted that there was no evidence that the persons involved had been aware of the Fugitive Slave Act, or that they "had any other intention than to protect one another from what they termed kidnappers." The jury left the court for their deliberations. They returned in about ten minutes with their verdict: not guilty. Ultimately, all charges against the Christiana prisoners were dropped.

The national attention showered on the Christiana events forced everyone — both north and south of the Mason-Dixon Line — to think more about the issues of freedom and slavery. It proved that the members of the black community in Lancaster County were not simply victims. They were people who willingly crossed geographical, philosophical, and even legal boundaries to assert their rights as human beings. Especially for them, the Mason-Dixon Line had become a symbol of freedom.

Harriet Tubman, a fugitive slave who risked her life many times leading others to freedom, eloquently stated how she felt when she first crossed the line: "When I found I had crossed that line, I looked at my hands to see if I was the same person. There was such a glory over every thing; the sun came like gold through the trees, and over the fields, and I felt like I was in Heaven."

As a legal boundary between slavery and freedom, Pennsylvania's 1780 Act for the Gradual Abolition of Slavery rang the early bells of the demise of slavery. Symbolically, Mason and Dixon's West Line, as a geographical boundary, reinforced the toll. Slaves who challenged the moral boundary of slavery and fought back by escaping rang the bells louder. The Civil War heralded the end to slavery. On January 1, 1863, President Abraham Lincoln issued the Emancipation Proclamation, an executive order that freed slaves in "States and parts of States wherein the people thereof respectively, are this

Harriet Tubman guided more than three hundred slaves to freedom.

SOUTH

NORTH

Mason' & Dixon's Line.

Highly unsuccessful Performance,
by Dismal Jemmy.

The first person to cross Niagara Falls on a tightrope did so in June 1860. This cartoon parodies President James Buchanan's unsuccessful attempts to politically balance the many disagreements between the North and the South.

day in rebellion against the United States." The states listed in the proclamation were Arkansas, Texas, Louisiana, Mississippi, Alabama, Florida, Georgia, South Carolina, North Carolina, and Virginia. But the proclamation did not free the slaves who lived south of the Mason-Dixon Line in Maryland or east of it, in Delaware. Both states had remained in the Union (Maryland under governmental force), where the proclamation did not apply. Neither would the proclamation free any of the slaves in the soon-to-be state of West Virginia, which was admitted to the Union in June 1863, with the gradual abolition of slavery already in its laws. Slavery did not officially end in the United States until the Thirteenth Amendment to the Constitution was adopted on December 6, 1865.

Since then, the Mason-Dixon Line, a reference once found peppering everyday talk, has largely become a topic mentioned only in history books and on highway signs along the border between Maryland and Pennsylvania. But the line has not been completely forgotten, nor should it be.

Chapter ✳ Thirteen

TIME'S BOUNDARY

LIKE PEOPLE LIVING in the mid-1800s, most people today perceive the Mason-Dixon Line as the boundary between the North and the South or between free and slave states. Some politicians and news media refer to it as the line between red states, which tend to support the Republican party in general elections, and blue states, which tend to support the Democratic party. That is, if they think of it at all. However, the Mason-Dixon Line should not be forgotten: it still *is* the boundary line separating Maryland, Delaware, and Pennsylvania. And some people *are* still interested in the line. For them, it has become a way to erase the boundary of time.

FINDING THE SOUTHERNMOST POINT — AGAIN

In the Old City area of Philadelphia, it's hard to walk more than a couple of blocks without seeing a historical marker. Philadelphia resident Janine Black wondered why no historical marker had been erected in her neighborhood, where the Plumstead-Huddle house had stood. After all, she figured, colonial officials had determined that the north wall of the house had been Philadelphia's southernmost point, and it was the spot where Mason and Dixon began their famous survey. In 2009, she contacted surveyor Todd Babcock, a founding member of the Mason & Dixon Line Preservation Partnership (MDLPP), an organization dedicated to locating, inventorying, and preserving the line's boundary stones. Babcock told Black that a historical marker could not be established unless a deed specifically describing the house's location could be found. And so far that hadn't happened.

Black, a college professor, sensed the search for the missing deed would be an interesting research project for students. That's how she met Indiah Fortune, Matthew McDermott, and Amanda Veloz. "Professor Black contacted my history professor, looking for students who could undertake a research project for her," McDermott recently recalled. "My professor told her I was a student who liked to hunt and sort through old files and was willing to dig for information. Our primary task was to find the location of a house that was no longer there."

When the three began their task at the Pennsylvania State Archives and the Pennsylvania Historical Society, they had no idea what to expect. "To begin the research," Fortune explained, "we looked through the Deed Book in the Philadelphia City Archives, which contained all the deeds during the 1700s that included either the Plumstead or Huddle surname. Janine provided us with a ton of information on what to look for while we were searching the old deeds. We were very careful while reviewing the deed book, because it was extremely aged and fragile. As a precaution, we tried to only touch the edges of the pages so they wouldn't deteriorate any further." They could handle some documents only while wearing white cotton gloves that protect old paper from the oils found on human skin.

Having been told that names were often spelled many different ways in colonial documents, the students decided to check all the deeds with variant spellings of Plumstead and Huddle. The list was long and quickly offered another stumbling block. "Reading eighteenth-century handwriting was no easy task," McDermott said with a laugh. "Words are spelled differently, the phrasing of language is not the same as we use, and the letter *s* when used in the middle of a word was shaped like the letter *f*. It took a while to get used to it." But, Fortune added, "the longer I looked at different deeds, the easier it became to understand."

The student researchers gradually zeroed in on their target. McDermott found a newspaper article from the 1860s that precisely described the location of the house. Then, in May 2010, Fortune found a 1754 deed for a house owned by Huddle. "When I realized that the deed I found had all the required information to be considered the first surveyed point of the Mason-Dixon Line, I was excited," recalled Fortune. "But I don't think it occurred to me how historic my discovery was until much later on." The site described on the deed matched that on another city record regarding the house's location. Several months later, Amanda Veloz found an insurance card that confirmed the Plumstead-Huddle house was located at the corner of Water Street and Cedar Street.

But hopes of exploring the home's site ended when Todd Babcock measured the neighborhood and discovered that the land where the house stood is now buried beneath the pavement of Interstate 95. Did the students feel that the search for the Plumstead-Huddle house — Mason and Dixon's starting point — had still been worth the time and effort? "It was all worth it," said McDermott. "Sometimes I read firsthand accounts written by Mason, Dixon, and William Penn's sons. Some of the papers still had candle-wax seals on them. It was unreal to see them. . . . Words can't describe how I felt." Fortune seconded

McDermott's thoughts: "This has been a truly amazing experience and I am so grateful to have been involved in such a monumental part of history. It was interesting to learn about the lives of different people during the colonial ages. Although my major has nothing to do with history, I've considered doing other historical research because of the great interest this project has sparked in me. This project has shown me that anyone can truly make a difference."

A NEW LOOK AT OLD STONES

At various times in the nineteenth and twentieth centuries, the state governments of Maryland, Pennsylvania, and Delaware hired surveyors to reconfirm their state boundaries. During those surveys, replacement boundary stones were set at some of the mileposts where Mason and Dixon's original stones had broken or disappeared. In 1952, a granite marker was placed at the site of the Post Marked West. Old family albums and library archives contain photographs of people posing with boundary stones, especially the original stones set by Mason and Dixon. Looking at these photos is like time traveling. In them, you can see some of the ways America has changed: in terms of the countryside, housing, and even fashion and hairstyles.

Here, a whole family, including the dog, poses for their own historic moment at a Mason-Dixon boundary stone.

Hikers, travelers, and anyone with a sense of adventure can visit the stones in person—with homeowner permission for those on privately owned land. Starting in 1990, Todd Babcock and the members of the Mason & Dixon Line Preservation Partnership undertook a mission to locate as many boundary stones as they could and assess their condition. In some ways, the modern hunt for the boundary stones resembled Mason and Dixon's venture. Like Mason and Dixon, Babcock and his colleagues spoke with landowners as they searched the line. They trekked

Despite wearing her Sunday best, this lady seems to have decided that the view—and perhaps the opportunity to stand on a historic monument—was worth the climb.

through fields and woods and occasionally splashed into rivers. In some places, they dug several feet of soil away from buried stones. The condition of the stones varied: some were in very good condition, while others had been chipped and gouged by farm machinery. Time had erased many of the crown stones' coats of arms, but the detail on a few was still crisp and easy to see. Landowners' stories led to the whereabouts of some of the seventy stones Mason and Dixon had left near Fort Frederick. As the years passed, local residents had hauled them away and used them for building. One is in a barn wall near Captain Evan Shelby's old house. Others became part of a house's walls, a door's threshold, and a porch step. In 1901, some were set as boundary markers during a confirming survey and maintenance check of the line.

Like a sentinel, crown stone 100, on the West Line, still remains steadfastly in place.

For as long as he can remember, the Mason-Dixon Line has been a part of Craig Babcock's life. He has spent countless days helping his father, Todd, locate and survey the boundary stones. Often, finding the stones was easier said than done. "I recall one being way back in the woods through swamps and briar bushes," Craig, now a college student, said. "We had several people looking and we fanned out through the woods to search for the stone, at times walking through mud, water, and even poison ivy. Another time, a stone was buried in a farmer's field and we had to dig several feet down to find it. Searching for them was memorable because, like in Mason and Dixon's days, it was an adventure. Digging in dirt and climbing through brush was fun, and finding the stone was a bonus." After a moment's reflection, he added, "The point of the trip is to find stones. But the trip isn't ruined if you don't. It's more about the experience of being out there, where Mason and Dixon walked and fought through that same brush you are fighting through. It's about hearing the stories of the people who live in the area and what their thoughts are, as well as other people who are involved in preserving the stones. Everyone has a story to bring and share, and that's what makes it exciting—not just saying you found a stone in the ground."

Craig Babcock's experience on the line helped him become an Eagle Scout. For his Eagle Scout project, he created his own stone inventory, locating stone mile markers along several highways in Berks County, Pennsylvania. He organized groups of scouts and friends to go out and locate the markers. "We created descriptions, gathered locations, and took pictures of the stones," he said. "I guess, in that way, I felt that I was doing something beneficial to the community and towards preserving a piece of history."

As the Babcocks explored the line, they often talked about how the survey was done. And they wondered, Was Mason and Dixon's line accurate within inches? They and other members of the Preservation Partnership double-checked the surveyors' accuracy with twenty-first-century technology: a global positioning system (GPS). "The stones that mark the line vary from the starting point by upwards of nine hundred feet," Todd Babcock said. But he has an explanation for why the surveyors periodically veered off the line: "I attribute this to the variation in gravity along the line, which had an impact on the plumb bob [of the zenith sector]. Gravity varies significantly along the line, and that was something they didn't fully understand and certainly had no way to correct." Gravity's effect depends on elevation, location, the mass of nearby mountains, and even on the density of the rock that underlies an area. The farther you are from the center of the earth (on a mountaintop, for example), the less the pull of gravity. (This was the hypothesis made by the Royal Society and supported by Mason and Dixon's observations of how the pendulum of

One of the milepost markers has been used as part of a concrete step in Pennsylvania.

Shelton's clock gained or lost time in John Harlan's garden.) While Mason and Dixon didn't climb mountains high enough to noticeably affect their results, the widespread locations where they made their astronomical observations did. "If the zenith sector's plumb bob were pulled from the vertical by varying amounts gravity along the boundary line, it would affect the readings taken on the zenith sector," Todd Babcock added. Babcock studied gravity's variations at Mason and Dixon's observation spots. He found that their deviations from the line of latitude correlated to the local variations in gravity. Limited by the eighteenth century's knowledge and understanding of gravity, Mason and Dixon's work establishing the line was as accurate as scientifically possible. Their work stands as an achievement that truly expanded the scientific boundaries of the eighteenth century. But do the boundaries of the Mason-Dixon Line hold any relevance for us today or for future generations?

THE LEGACY

The story of the Mason-Dixon Line is a tapestry of boundaries: territorial and religious, scientific and cultural, economic and moral. The many boundary journeys found in the complete story of the Mason-Dixon Line are relevant today. They ask us to understand why certain historical events happened. They ask us to examine what happened as the result of these events. They prompt us to question motivations and actions and to recognize similar patterns occurring in our world today.

The Mason-Dixon Line's story introduces people whose boundary journeys converged in America. Here they created and shaped a country with its own set of boundaries. Although the journey is still tough for some, all individuals in America are guaranteed the freedom to explore, challenge, change, and defend these boundaries. It is the responsibility of all Americans to do so. When we accept this responsibility, we connect with the hopes, ambitions, and lives of those who came before us. We accept the challenge of keeping their dreams alive. In this way, we, like the Mason-Dixon Line, will create a legacy that will affect the lives of future people.

Epilogue

WHOLE BOOKS have been written about some of the partici-pants in the saga of Mason and Dixon's line, the Calvert and Penn families among them. You can easily find them in libraries. But many of the people (and the instruments!) who played a role in Mason and Dixon's American adventure have slipped through documentary cracks in the historical record and disappeared. Or perhaps they remain lost in archives, just waiting for an adventure-seeking researcher to find them, like the information recently rediscovered about the Plumstead-Huddle house. However, records that have already come to light offer tantalizing glimpses about what happened to certain people (and instru-ments) who participated in the survey. Many of these glimpses raise more questions. . . .

CHARLES MASON observed the 1769 transit of Venus, in Ireland, for the Royal Society. (After completing their survey in America, Mason and Dixon did not work together again.) He continued his astronomi-cal work and was highly regarded for creating a set of lunar and solar tables. But he never forgot his time in America. In September 1786, Mason, Mary (his second wife), seven sons, and a daughter immigrated to Philadelphia. Less than two weeks after their arrival, he sent a note to

Benjamin Franklin, informing him that he was sick and confined to bed. Sadly, Mason died less than a month later, on October 25, 1786. He is buried in an unmarked grave in Christ Church Burial Ground, not far from the tall steeple he first saw when he entered Philadelphia in 1763. Several Pennsylvania newspapers published his obituary.

JEREMIAH DIXON also observed the 1769 transit of Venus, but in Norway. Afterward, he worked as a surveyor in England. Several years later, he bought a dyehouse, which provided him with additional income. Dixon never married. He died on January 22, 1779, at the age of forty-six. The location of his grave is unknown. In his will, he left the rent and profits of the dyehouse to Margaret Bland, instructing that she use them "for and towards the maintenance, education, and bringing up of her two daughters, Mary and Elizabeth." The dyehouse was to belong to Mary and Elizabeth when they reached the age of twenty-one. The relationship between Margaret, her daughters, and Jeremiah Dixon is unknown.

MOSES MCCLEAN served as a captain during the Revolutionary War. He became a prisoner of war after being captured by Indians who sided with the British. He remarried after his wife, Sarah—whom Charles Mason had met—died. He and his second wife moved to Ohio. Moses died in 1810.

JOHN HARLAN is reported in the Harlan family genealogy as having drowned in Brandywine Creek. His name ceases to appear in colonial records after 1768.

PHINEHAS HARLAN married his sweetheart, Elizabeth Jones, on September 24, 1766, one year after he worked as an axman on the line.

THOMAS AND HANNAH CRESAP remained loyal Marylanders. By the mid-1740s, Thomas established a fort and trading post along the bank of the Potomac River, in the wilderness of western Maryland, and within a few years built the home Mason and Dixon visited. When George Washington was sixteen years old and participating in a frontier land survey, he spent two nights at the Cresaps' home. In his journal, Washington wrote that the road to Cresap's house was "I believe the Worst Road that ever was trod by Man or Beast." Cresap and his son became land speculators and founded the town of Oldtown. Hannah Cresap died before 1774. Thomas died in 1790; his grave overlooks the Potomac River. Yet his spirit of discovery lives on in the archaeological excavations on the site of Cresap's fort, where an abundance of eighteenth-century artifacts have been unearthed.

ZENITH SECTOR: Owned by the Penn family, the sector remained in Pennsylvania. It was used to observe the 1769 transit of Venus and to survey the boundary between New York and New Jersey. After the Revolutionary War, the sector was housed in different cities, and eventually put on display in the Pennsylvania state capitol building, in Harrisburg. It was reported as destroyed when the building burned in February 1897.

TRANSIT AND EQUAL ALTITUDE INSTRUMENT: For many years, the transit's whereabouts were unknown. Then, in 1912, it was found in Philadelphia underneath the floorboards in the bell tower of Independence Hall, formerly called the Pennsylvania State House, the building where Mason and Dixon sometimes met with the commissioners. How the instrument got there no one knows. It is on display in a large meeting room in the hall, possibly the same room where Mason and Dixon first unpacked it in 1763.

AUTHOR'S NOTE

AMERICAN HISTORY is one of my favorite topics, so research-ing the material for this book was like going on a treasure hunt. I began my search believing, as most people do, that the Mason-Dixon Line had something to do with the Missouri Compromise and the Civil War. As I dug deeper, my perception changed considerably. I learned that individuals — ordinary folks like you and me — dared to cross many different kinds of boundaries, and in doing so shaped a nation. They prove that one person with a dream can change the world.

People I met during my research journey greatly enriched my story of the line. Todd Babcock steered me toward Moses McClean's account book in the archives at the Historical Society of Pennsylvania. McClean's lists added depth to the story and gave names to otherwise unknown crewmen. Todd patiently answered questions about surveying, as did Matthew Parbs and Robert Church at the National Museum of Surveying, in Springfield, Illinois. Surveyor and historian Jack Owens shed a clear, much-needed light onto the intricacies of running the Tangent Line and taught me how to use a level and a Gunter's chain. Edwin Danson's book *Drawing the Line* helped me understand the mystery of the Tangent Line. Craig Babcock took time from his busy back-to-college schedule and shared some of his experiences on the line. It's likely that he has worked harder on the line and touched more of its boundary stones than any kid of his generation. At the American Philosophical Society, in Philadelphia, Roy Goodman kindly steered me through their Mason and Dixon files. Also in Philadelphia, Karie Diethorn took me upstairs at Independence Hall so I could see Dixon's transit and equal altitude instrument. Deborah Warner, at the Smithsonian Institute, in Washington, D.C., explained how a zenith sector worked; she and Peter Marques, of Tentsmiths, provided me with information about eighteenth-century tents.

The Boundary Commissioners, the Calverts and Penns, and the governors of Pennsylvania and Maryland left a rich trail of documents. Deciding which snippets to include wasn't easy, because I loved them all. In the end, I chose material that helped me better understand people and their reasons for pushing the boundaries of their world. Prior to researching this book, I thought William Penn was as dry as dust. After reading his writings and the transcript of his trial, I now see him as an earnest man of commitment, integrity, intelligence, honor, and dry wit. Period portraits and sketches put faces to the names of some folks in this book. Frustratingly, there are no images of Mason and Dixon. Before I began my research, in my mind's eye I pictured them as old. I was startled when I realized that when Dixon began surveying the line, he was the same age my son was when he and I visited the Harlan farm and the Stargazer's Stone. The ages of the boundary-line crewmen surprised me as well: a few were teenagers, and most were in their twenties or thirties.

At the fork of the Brandywine, Kate Roby graciously spent an afternoon showing my son and me around the Harlan house. She shared many family tales. Sitting in rooms that Mason and Dixon had often occupied, I understood why they kept coming back. Linda Kaat, who lives less than a stone's throw from Joel Baily's house, filled me in on the importance of taverns as colonial newsrooms.

Professor Janine Black and students Indiah Fortune, Amanda Veloz, and Matthew McDermott shared their modern-day quest for the location of the Plumstead-Huddle house, in Philadelphia. For them, one question started a journey of many twists, turns, and dead ends. But it was a journey that ultimately ended with the satisfaction of success. I agree with Matthew: you feel a special connection with the people of the past when you hold an old handwritten document. It's a connection that erases time.

Stars are among the "stars" of this book. Matt Wiesner, at the observatory at Northern Illinois University, showed me a whole new world. Visiting the observatory on nights during different seasons helped me understand how Earth's daily and annual rotations affect the stars we see. Perhaps most thrilling was watching the 2012 transit of Venus. It was an incredible coincidence that this astronomically rare event should occur while I was researching this book—and that I saw it, just like Mason and Dixon. Thankfully, no French warships sailed across Illinois's horizons.

Seventeenth-century Maryland comes alive in Historic Saint Mary's City. I easily imagined Leonard Calvert and the 1634 colonists disembarking from the *Ark* and *Dove*. A research trip to London took me to the Tower of London, where William Penn was imprisoned. I stood in the church where he was baptized and walked on the grounds where he played as a boy. Seeing Jeremiah Dixon's circumferentor and the Shelton clock that Mason and Dixon used for their experiment in John Harlan's garden helped me better understand how they worked. While being in London was exciting, my journey along part of the West Line was equally so. As my husband and I cleared stinging nettles away from one crown stone, we learned why the plant got its name — and not to touch it again. We walked some of the hilly terrain the crew had traveled — they definitely got their exercise! In one rural wooded area, I was afraid we might see a snake, but white-tailed deer were the only animals we encountered. (Being familiar with that area of Pennsylvania, I just *know* that Mason and Dixon must have seen at least one rattlesnake.)

I love letting my imagination roam as I meander in places like Saint Mary's City, the fork of the Brandywine, and Philadelphia. On October 25, 2012, the 226th anniversary of Charles Mason's death, I wandered among the gravestones in Christ Church Burial Ground. In all these places, a whisper of those who came before us lingers. These years-old whispers always inspire me. A million questions flood my mind. I have a burning desire to learn more. And so begins another adventure.

Although Mason and Dixon initially used a canvas observatory tent, carpenters soon constructed a more substantial wooden one, similar to this reconstruction set up at the Surveyors Rendezvous in August 2013. Instruments would have rested on stable bases constructed inside. The observatory was easily disassembled by removing the wood pegs. Wagons hauled the stacked wall and roof panels.

SOURCE NOTES

CHAPTER 1: OLD-WORLD PREJUDICE, NEW-WORLD DREAMS

p. 2: "evil in religion": Krugler, p. 28.

p. 4: "20. and odd Negroes": Sluiter, pp. 395–398.

p. 4: "the dear companion and only comfort": Krugler, p. 70.

p. 6: "from the middst . . . of them dyed" and "I am determined . . . to deserve it": Proceedings of the Council of Maryland, 1636–1667, vol. 3, p. 16.

CHAPTER 2: MARYLAND'S SHORES

p. 9: "which lieth under . . . New England ends": Charter of Maryland.

p. 11: "to preserve unity . . . or in England," "be done as privately as may be," and "treate the Protestants . . . Justice will permitt": Hall, p. 16.

p. 12: "the most delightfull water I ever saw," "At our first . . . all the Country," and "came in a . . . unto them all": Ibid., p. 40.

p. 13: "gave leave to . . . where we pleased": Ibid., p. 41.

p. 13: "axes, hoes, cloth and hatchets": Ibid., p. 42.

pp. 14–15: "The cedar you . . . usefull tymber trees": Ibid., p. 158.

CHAPTER 3: CONVICTIONS AND CONSCIENCE

p. 25: "could not contain himself from weeping aloud" and "saw the tears running down his cheeks": Peare, p. 23.

pp. 25–26: "Imbroidery and diamonds . . . so much overcome" and "both the King . . . at the window": Pepys, vol. 2, pp. 82–83.

p. 26: "He, with certain . . . pray'd amongst themselves": Penn, vol. 1, p. 1.

p. 26: "endeavoured by both Words and Blows" and "turn'd him out of Doors": Ibid., p. 2.

p. 27: "a great deal . . . will signify little": Pepys, vol. 5, p. 257.

p. 28: "Preach and Speak": Penn, vol. 1, p. 9.

pp. 28–29: "Because I do not . . . be any Respect," "Contempt of the Court," "I desire it . . . should be fined," "I desire you . . . ground my Indictment," and "the Common-Law": Ibid., p. 11.

p. 29: "The Question is . . . there is no Transgression": Ibid., p. 12.

pp. 29–30: "Gentlemen, you shall . . . starve for it," "should be Free, and not Compelled," "You are Englishmen . . . away your Right," and "Nor will we ever do it": Ibid., p. 15.

CHAPTER 4: THE SEED OF A NATION

p. 32: "a profitable plantation to the crown": Soderlund, p. 23.

p. 32: "to extend Westwards . . . New Castle" and "by a straight . . . Longitude above mentioned": Pennsylvania Charter.

p. 34: "the seed of a nation" and "God has given . . . oppress his person": Soderlund, p. 55.

p. 35: "So farewell to . . . but remains forever" Ibid., p. 170.

p. 36: Richard Townsend . . . needs with care: Peare, pp. 245–246.

p. 38: "about 80 houses . . . above 300 farms settled": Soderlund, p. 292.

CHAPTER 5: WHOSE LAND?

p. 40: "strainger in the affaires of the Country," "the business of the bounds," "observing our just limitts," and "Just & friendly": Calvert Papers, vol. 1, pp. 322–323.

p. 40: "pay any more taxes . . . law of Maryland": Soderlund, p. 79.

p. 42: "But as the Line . . . Southward of them": Minutes of the Provincial Council of Pennsylvania, vol. 3, p. 470.

p. 44: "so long as he behaves . . . Friendship with the Indians": Proceedings of the Council of Maryland, 1732–1753, vol. 28, p. 7.

p. 45: "he lived in the Jurisdiction . . . no right to be there": Pennsylvania Archives, series 1, vol. 1, p. 398.

p. 45: "If the Lord Baltimore . . . Apply to the King," "they have . . . Penn was their King," "being or pretending to be Inhabitants of Pennsylvania," "Riotous manner Armed . . . Weapons," and "Ten pounds Current Money of this our Province": Proceedings of the Council of Maryland, 1732–1753, vol. 28, pp. 21–22.

p. 46: "have offered large . . . house on fire": Ibid., p. 69.

p. 46: "came with about twenty . . . Blunderbusses & Drum beating": Pennsylvania Archives, series 1, vol. 1, p. 465.

p. 46: "armed with guns, pistols, and swords": Calvert Papers, microfilm reel 21, no. 319.

p. 46: "high Crimes & Misdemeanors": Pennsylvania Archives, series 1, vol. 1, p. 489.

p. 47: "they would not depart . . . dead or alive": Calvert Papers, microfilm reel 21, no. 319.

p. 47: "Quakeing Dogs & Rogues": Pennsylvania Archives, series 1, vol. 1, p. 505.

p. 47: "who was very big . . . with the Fright": Calvert Papers, microfilm reel 21, no. 319.

p. 47: "This is one of the Prettyest Towns in Maryland": Pennsylvania Archives, series 1, vol. 1, p. 510.

p. 48: "the Governors . . . Borders of their respective Provinces": Proceedings of the Council of Maryland, 1732–1753, vol. 28, pp. 130–131.

p. 48: "Nothing is more certain . . . perpetually to quarrell": Pennsylvania Archives, series 1, vol. 1, p. 483.

p. 50: "This morning our Workmen . . . enlarge their wages" and "till late at night often to the mid-thigh in water": Calvert Papers, microfilm reel 22, no. 469.

p. 51: "I pray to be released . . . Lenth of 80 miles": Lukens to Peters, June 16, 1762, Chew Family Papers, collection 2050, box 25, folder 64.

p. 52: "three different offsets of the line": Lukens to Peters, August 29, 1762, Ibid.

CHAPTER 6: STARS IN THEIR EYES

p. 60: "We wait for nothing but a fair wind": Mason and Dixon to Thomas Birch, November 24, 1760, American Philosophical Society, Mason and Dixon Papers, B. M381.

p. 60: "Our loss amounts to 11 killed . . . her Hull much wounded" and "take up so much time . . . Observations upon the Transit": Dixon to Birch, January 12, 1761, Ibid.

p. 60: "easily turned to any part of the heavens": Mason, C. and J. Dixon, Philosophical Transactions of the Royal Society, 1761: vol. 52, p. 379.

p. 60: tarred the top . . . joints with putty: Expense receipt, Charles Mason to Nevil Maskelyne, January 2, 1762, American Philosophical Society, Mason and Dixon Papers, B. M381.

p. 61: "Persons intirely accomplished & of good character" and "settle & Determine": Correspondence of Governor Sharpe, vol. 14, p. 106.

CHAPTER 7: SURVEYORS TO THE RESCUE

p. 63: hired two horses: Cash Paid Out by Mason, Chew Family Papers, collection 2050, box 20, folder 20.

p. 65: "landing and carriage": Ibid.

pp. 66–67: "Danger from the Incursions of the Indians" and "if the Business . . . naturally low and wet": Pennsylvania Commissioners to Thomas and Richard Penn, December 21, 1763, Chew Family Papers, collection 2050, box 25, folder 18.

p. 68: "made accessible . . . as soon as possible," "use their best . . . Penns or Calvert," and "You are to enter fair minutes . . . which the lines may pass": Minutes and papers of the Mason and Dixon survey, 1760–1768, vol. 1, December 5, 6, and 9, 1763.

p. 68: "violent storm": Mason expense account, December 17, 1763, Chew Family Papers, collection 2050, box 20, folder 20.

p. 70: "entirely peaceable and . . . as the whites were": Barber journal.

p. 78: "inhumanly killed six of the Indians": *Pennsylvania Gazette*, January 5, 1764, p. 2.

p. 78: "Muskets, Tomahawks, & Scalping knives." Edward Shippen to Joseph Shippen, January 5, 1764, Shippen Papers, file B Sh62.

p. 79: "Gentleman: I hope . . . and an agreeable companion": Richard Peters to Mason, January 7, 1764, Mason's Journal, p. 38.

p. 80: "put [it] with the rest of our Instruments into the wagons" and "carried on the Springs . . . of a single Horse chair [carriage]": Mason's Journal, January 11, 1764, p. 38.

p. 80: "Finding we were very near . . . Erect the Observatory": Ibid., January 16, 1764, p. 39.

pp. 80–81: "I've here the pleasure . . . Labourers will then be wanted" and "When I left Philadelphia . . . always be acknowledg'd": Mason to Richard Peters, January 27, 1764, Chew Papers, collection 2050, box 26, folder 2.

p. 81: "flying clouds": Mason's Journal, March 5, 1764, p. 45.

p. 82: "The edge of the Sun's Shadow . . . the best defined I ever saw": Ibid., March 18, 1764, p. 45.

CHAPTER 8: TACKLING THE IMPOSSIBLE

p. 83: "visto in the Meridian Southward": Mason's Journal, March 19, 1764, p. 45.

p. 87: "Proved the Meridian and found it very exact" and "Found the chain a little too long. Corrected it": Ibid., April 5, 1764, p. 47.

p. 90: "five Laborers in carrying one of the instruments": Ibid., April 18, 1764, p. 48.

p. 92: reward for them in the *Pennsylvania Gazette*: *Pennsylvania Gazette*, June 16, 1763, p. 3.

p. 102: "To prove that the Chain Carriers . . . Link of the same": Mason's Journal, August 27, 1764, p. 60.

p. 102: "There is the greatest quantity . . . reach the clouds": Ibid., September 13, 1764, p. 63.

p. 106: "it was so near a right angle . . . true tangent Point" and "what we had done . . . stand as finished": Ibid., November 13, 1764, p. 66.

CHAPTER 9: THE WEST LINE

pp. 107–108: "What brought me here . . . none alive to tell" and "Strange it was . . . no honor to them!": Mason's Journal, January 10, 1765, p. 66.

p. 108: "one Mr. Crisep . . . with about 55" and "would not surrender . . . lost his life coming out": Ibid., January 17, 1765, p. 67.

p. 109: "Met some boys . . . as if all had been well": Ibid., February 24, 1765, p. 67.

p. 110: "the Stamp Act . . . First of November next": *Pennsylvania Gazette*, June 20, 1765, p. 2.

p. 110: "which the fatal and never-to-be-forgotten Stamp-Act": *South Carolina Gazetteer; and Country Journal*, "City of New York," December 17, 1765, p. 4.

p. 111: "not to buy any goods . . . the Stamp Act shall be repealed": Ibid.

p. 114: "[As] I was returning . . . Cloud to the Horizon": Mason's Journal, May 27, 1765, p. 87.

p. 115: "in the same manner . . . country is inhabited": Ibid., June 18, 1765, p. 92.

p. 116: "one inch and six tenths in Length . . . half an inch thick": Ibid., August 8, 1765, p. 100.

p. 116: "the Taking [of] frequent Observations . . . Line by many Miles": Correspondence of Governor Sharpe, vol. 14, pp. 199–200.

pp. 117–119: "Immediately there opens a room . . . support nature's arch)," "On the sidewalls . . . Monuments of a Temple," "Striking its Visitants . . . numbered as one of them," "a fine river of water," and "other rooms, but not so large as the first": Mason's Journal, September 22, 1765, p. 111.

p. 119: "by its appearance . . . direction of our Line": Ibid., October 27, 1765, p. 117.

p. 120: "and left them . . . at Captain Shelby's": Ibid., October 26, 1765, p. 115.

p. 121: the team would need between fifty and sixty crown stones and about two hundred regular mile markers: Correspondence of Governor Sharpe, vol. 14, pp. 216–217.

CHAPTER 10: CONTINUING WEST

p. 123: "on the whole . . . Cash to proceed with": Correspondence of Governor Sharpe, vol. 14, p. 298.

p. 124: "oak and hickory buds just breaking into Leaf": Mason's Journal, March 11, 1766, p. 121.

pp. 124–126: "Boundary between the Natives . . . his Britanic Majesties Collonies," "the best . . . of North America," "The Rivers abound . . . quantity almost increditable," and "From the solitary tops . . . spirit that made them": Ibid., June 14, 1766, p. 129.

p. 126: forty-one wagonloads of oats and Indian corn: *Pennsylvania Gazette,* May 22, 1755, p. 4.

p. 127: "Our numbers consisted . . . prey to the Enemy": Washington to Robert Dinwiddie, July 18, 1755, George Washington Papers, Letter book 1.

p. 128: "dismal inhospitable Place": Pennsylvania Archives, series 1, vol. 2, 1755, p. 309.

p. 128: "made through the desert . . . never to return" and "beautifully situated on a rising ground": Mason's Journal, June 22, 1766, p. 129.

pp. 128–129: "measured three leaves . . . 12 inches in breadth": Ibid., July 6, 1766, p. 130.

p. 130: "proceed immediately . . . in the [West] Line": Ibid., October 29, 1766, p. 147.

CHAPTER 11: DANGEROUS TERRITORY

p. 133: "the limbs of the Trees . . . clear Ice upon them": Mason's Journal, January 27, 1767, p. 155.

p. 134: "all the Chief Sackems and principal Warriors of the Six Nations": William Johnson Papers, vol. 5, p. 486.

p. 135: "from their desire . . . for their attendance": Ibid., vol. 12, pp. 309–310.

p. 137: "to make the [Indians] a small present . . . for their trouble" and "to use his utmost . . . to return home": Minutes of the Boundary Commission, June 22, 1767.

p. 138: "As the public Peace . . . other persons whatsoever": commissioners to Mason and Dixon, June 18, 1767, Mason's Journal, p. 177.

p. 138: "the tallest man I ever saw": Memoranda, 1767, Mason's Journal, p. 174.

pp. 138–140: "we are all . . . and friendly Manner" and "left us . . . required them at Home": Mason and Dixon to Benjamin Chew, August 25, 1767, Chew Family Papers, collection 2050, box 26, folder 3.

p. 140: "through which you may travel . . . not find one Hill": Memoranda, 1767, Mason's Journal, p. 176.

p. 141: "WANTED, Able bodied Negroe . . . and a garden, rent free": *Pennsylvania Gazette,* various issues, March 22, 1764, to December 24, 1767.

p. 144: "found plenty of fish . . . particularly cat fish": Memoranda, 1767, Mason's Journal, p. 174.

p. 145: "Chief of the Delaware Nation": Ibid.

p. 146: "with Blankets and . . . Bows and Arrows": Ibid., p. 175.

p. 146: "This day the Chief . . . one step farther Westward": Mason's Journal, October 9, 1767, p. 187.

pp. 146–148: "Suppressed part of what he might have informed you": William Johnson Papers, vol. 6, pp. 71–73.

p. 148: "had a great mind . . . his own Country": Memoranda, 1767, Mason's Journal, p. 175.

p. 148: "On the top of . . . five feet High": Mason's Journal, October 18, 1767, p. 190.

p. 149: "a silk handkerchief sent to his widow": Joseph Shippen Accounts, Chew Family Papers, collection 2050, box 20, folder 3.

p. 149: "decently buried": William Johnson Papers, vol. 6, p. 6.

pp. 149–150: "acted very prudently in refusing to give the extravagant Price": Chew to Mason and Dixon, November 6, 1767, Chew Family Papers, collection 2050 box 25, folder 11.

p. 150: "In all the Mountains . . . superior to those sent from England" and "The Marks we have erected . . . to destroy them": Mason to Hugh Hamersley, January 29, 1768, Calvert Papers 174, microfilm reel 26, no. 1311.

p. 150: venison, corn pudding, and turnips: Mason and Dixon's expense account, February 1767 to December 24, 1767, Chew Family Papers, collection 2050, box 20, folder 20.

p. 151: "to put an end to this tedious Business": Mason's Journal, p. 192.

p. 151: "no further occasion . . . Honorable Proprietors": Ibid., December 26, 1767, p. 194.

p. 151: "But the Earth is not . . . this as accurate": Ibid., January 8, 1768, p. 194.

p. 152: "Keep the rods . . . to your Labourers": Ibid., p. 136.

p. 155: "Thus ends my restless progress in America": Ibid., September 11, 1768, p. 211.

CHAPTER 12: FREEDOM'S BOUNDARY

p. 157: "I wish they would compromise . . . our [Virginia] assembly": Thomas Jefferson to Edmund Pendleton, August, 26, 1776.

p. 158: "The storm then took . . . Mason and Dixon did": *Freeman's Journal*, July 7, 1784.

p. 159: "What Sir, patronize our . . . employ John Bull": *Connecticut Courant*, vol. 69, no. 3570, p. 1.

p. 159: "in obedience to . . . Abolition of Slavery'": Pennsylvania Archives, Cumberland County, Clerk of Court-Slave Returns Inventory.

p. 160: Between 1780 and 1782, 6,855 slaves lived in Pennsylvania; in 1810, that number had been reduced to 795: Nash and Soderlund, p. 5.

p. 161: only 10 percent of Maryland's slaveholders owned eight or more slaves: Slaughter, p. 6.

p. 162: In 1849, more free blacks . . . in any other state: Historical Census Browser, University of Virginia Library, http://mapserver.lib.virginia.edu/php/state.php.

p. 162: Between June 1849 and June 1850, 279 slaves escaped from Maryland: Slaughter, p. 17.

p. 162: "obey and execute all warrants . . . issued under the provisions of this act" and "In no trial . . . which he escaped": Fugitive Slave Act, amended as part of the Compromise of 1850.

p. 165: "You have my property," "Go in the room . . . them are yours," and "They are not mine . . . bound to have them": Parker, pp. 283–284.

p. 165: "set the house on fire, and burn them up": Ibid., p. 284.

p. 166: a reasonable estimate is about twenty-five: Member of the Philadelphia Bar, p. 37.

p. 167: "I have stood . . . blessings of freedom": "Frederick Douglass' Address." *The North Star*, vol. 1., no. 32, p. 2.

p. 167: "If it be right . . . of all man's rights": *Frederick Douglass' Paper*, September 25, 1851.

p. 168: "I shook hands . . . Liberty at Christiana" and "this affair . . . fugitive slave bill": Douglass, p. 350.

p. 168: "of previous conspiracy . . . of the United States" and "had any other intention . . . they termed kidnappers": Member of the Philadelphia Bar, p. 80.

p. 169: "When I found . . . I was in Heaven": Bradford, p. 19. Words spelled phonetically by Bradford to reflect dialect have been corrected for clarity.

CHAPTER 13: TIME'S BOUNDARY

p. 172: "Professor Black contacted . . . no longer there": Telephone call with the author, July 22, 2011.

p. 172: "To begin the research . . . deteriorate any further": E-mail correspondence with the author, July 27, 2011.

p. 173: "Reading eighteenth-century handwriting . . . to get used to it": Telephone conversation with the author, July 22, 2011.

p. 173: "The longer I looked . . . it became to understand": E-mail correspondence with the author, July 27, 2011.

p. 173: "When I realized . . . until much later on": E-mail correspondence with the author, July 27, 2011.

p. 173: "It was all worth it . . . describe how I felt": Telephone conversation with the author, July 22, 2011.

p. 174: "This has been a truly . . . make a difference": E-mail correspondence with the author, July 27, 2011.

pp. 176–177: "I recall one . . . stone was a bonus," "The point of the trip . . . stone in the ground," and "We created descriptions . . . of history": E-mail correspondence with the author, August 24, 2012.

pp. 177–178: "The stones that mark . . . nine hundred feet," "I attribute this . . . no way to correct," and "If the zenith sector's . . . taken on the zenith sector": E-mail correspondence with author, August 27, 2012.

EPILOGUE

p. 181: "for and towards the maintenance . . . Mary and Elizabeth": Jeremiah Dixon's will.

p. 182: "I believe the Worst Road . . . by Man or Beast": Jackson and Twohig, vol. 1, p. 12.

BIBLIOGRAPHY

PRIMARY SOURCES

Barber, Rhoda. "Journal of Settlement at Wright's Ferry on Susquehanna River." Handwritten manuscript, Historical Society of Pennsylvania.

Calvert Papers. Historical Society of Maryland (microfilm) and Library of Congress, American Memory. http://memory.loc.gov/ammem/index.htm.

Charter of Maryland. Maryland State Archives, Microfilm MSA SC M3145, p. 15. Also online at http://www.msa.md.gov/megafile/msa/speccol/sc4800/sc4872/003145/html/m3145-0012 .html.

Chew Family Papers. Historical Society of Pennsylvania.

Correspondence of Governor Sharpe. Maryland State Archives.

Emancipation Proclamation, January 1, 1863. National Archives & Records Administration. http://www.archives.gov/exhibits/featured_documents/emancipation_proclamation /transcript.html. The original handwritten text can be viewed at http://www.archives.gov /exhibits/featured_documents/emancipation_proclamation/index.html.

"Frederick Douglass's Address." *The North Star* 1, no. 32: 2.

Frederick Douglass' Paper. Accessible Archives, Northern Illinois University Library.

George Washington Papers, 1741–1799: Series 2 Letterbooks. Library of Congress, American Memory. http://memory.loc.gov/ammem/index.htm.

Jeremiah Dixon's will. The Mason & Dixon Line Preservation Partnership. http://www.mdlpp.org.

Mason, Charles. The Journal of Charles Mason and Jeremiah Dixon. Transcribed by A. Hughlett Mason. Memoirs of the American Philosophical Society, vol. 76, 1969. Philadelphia: American Philosophical Society. Mason's handwritten journal is digitized and available online at National Archives Online Public Access: Minutes and Papers of the Mason and Dixon Survey, 1760–1768. National Archives and Records Administration. http://research .archives.gov/description/5821514.

Minutes of the Boundary Commission. American Philosophical Society, Philadelphia.

Minutes of the Provincial Council of Pennsylvania. Philadelphia: Jos. Severns, 1852. New York: AMS Press, 1968, vols. 3 and 9. Also Pennsylvania Archives: Colonial Records, http://www .fold3.com.

Pennsylvania Archives: [1st ser.]: selected and arranged from original documents in the Office of the Secretary of the Commonwealth, conformably to acts of the General Assembly, February 15, 1851, and March 1, 1852. Edited by Samuel Hazard. Vols. 1 and 2. Philadelphia: Jos. Severns, 1852.

Pennsylvania Archives, Cumberland County, Clerk of Court-Slave Returns Inventory. George Stevenson, 1780.050. http://records.ccpa.net/weblink_public_print/DocView .aspx?id=237572&dbid=7.

Pennsylvania Charter. Pennsylvania Historical & Museum Commission. http://www.portal.state .pa.us/portal/server.pt/community/documents_from_1681_-_1776,_colonial_days/20421 /pennsylvania_charter/998169.

Pennsylvania Gazette. Accessible Archives, Northern Illinois University Library.

Proceedings of the Council of Maryland. Archives of Maryland Online. http://msa.maryland .gov/megafile/msa/speccol/sc2900/sc2908/html/volumes.html.

Shippen Papers. American Philosophical Society.

South Carolina Gazetteer; and Country Journal

Thomas Jefferson to Edmund Pendleton. August 26, 1776. University of Nebraska–Lincoln, Center for Digital Research in the Humanities. http://jeffersonswest.unl.edu/archive/view _doc.php?id=jef.00099.

William Johnson Papers. New York State Library digital edition, 2008. http://nysl.nysed.gov/uhtbin /cgisirsi/20120812192457/SIRSI/0/518/0/423659/Content/1?new_gateway_db=ILINK.

BOOKS

Bailey, Kenneth P. *Thomas Cresap: Maryland Frontiersman.* Boston: Christopher Publishing House, 1944.

Bradford, Sarah H. *Scenes in the Life of Harriet Tubman.* Auburn, NY: W. J. Moses, 1869.

Brubaker, Jack. *Massacre of the Conestogas: On the Trail of the Paxton Boys in Lancaster County.* Charleston, SC: History Press, 2010.

Cummings, Hubertis M. *The Mason and Dixon Line, Story for a Bicentenary, 1763–1963.* Harrisburg, PA: Commonwealth of Pennsylvania, Dept. of Internal Affairs, 1962.

Danson, Edwin. *Drawing the Line: How Mason and Dixon Surveyed the Most Famous Border in America.* New York: Wiley, 2001.

DePree, Christopher, and Alan Axelrod. *The Complete Idiot's Guide to Astronomy.* New York: Alpha Books, 1999.

Douglass, Frederick. *Life and Times of Frederick Douglass.* Hartford: Park Publishing, 1881.

Dunn, Mary Maples, and Richard S. Dunn, eds. *The Papers of William Penn.* Vols. 1 and 2. Philadelphia: University of Pennsylvania Press, 1981 and 1982.

Ecenbarger, William. *Walkin' the Line: A Journey from Past to Present along the Mason-Dixon.* New York: M. Evans, 2000.

Fantel, Hans. *William Penn: Apostle of Dissent.* New York: Morrow, 1974.

Hall, Clayton Colman, ed. *Narratives of Early Maryland, 1633–1684.* New York: Scribner's, 1910.

Hensel, W. U. *The Christiana Riot and the Treason Trials of 1851.* 1911. Reprint. New York: Negro Universities Press, 1969.

Heywood, Linda M., and John K. Thornton. *Central Africans, Atlantic Creoles, and the Foundation of the Americas, 1585–1660.* New York: Cambridge University Press, 2007.

Jackson, Donald, and Dorothy Twohig, eds. *The Diaries of George Washington*. Vol. 1. Charlottesville: University Press of Virginia, 1976. http://memory.loc.gov/ammem/gwhtml/gwhome.html.

Kenny, Kevin. *Peaceable Kingdom Lost: The Paxton Boys and the Destruction of William Penn's Holy Experiment*. New York: Oxford University Press, 2009.

Krugler, John D. *English and Catholic: The Lords Baltimore in the Seventeenth Century*. Baltimore: Johns Hopkins University Press, 2004.

Land, Aubrey C. *Colonial Maryland, a History*. New York: KTO Press, 1981.

Member of the Philadelphia Bar. *A History of the Trial of Castner Hanway and Others for Treason at Philadelphia in November, 1851*. Philadelphia: Uriah Hunt & Sons, 1852. http://archive.org /details/historyoftrialof00memb.

Moché, Dinah L. *Astronomy: A Self-Teaching Guide*. New York: Wiley, 2000.

Moore, Patrick. *Exploring the Night Sky with Binoculars*. New York: Cambridge University Press, 2000.

Nash, Gary B., and Jean R. Soderlund. *Freedom by Degrees: Emancipation in Pennsylvania and Its Aftermath*. New York: Oxford University Press, 1991.

Peare, Catherine Owens. *William Penn: a Biography*. Philadelphia: Lippincott, 1957.

Penn, William. *A Collection of the Works of William Penn, to Which Is Prefixed a Journal of His Life, with Many Original Letters and Papers Not before Published*. London: J. Sowle, 1726. Vol. 1, The Author's Life, p. 1. http://archive.org/stream/collectionofwork01penn#page/n0/mode/2up.

Pepys, Samuel. *The Diary of Samuel Pepys*. Edited by Robert Latham and William Matthews. Berkeley: University of California Press, 1983.

Riordan, Timothy B. *The Plundering Time: Maryland and the English Civil War, 1645–1646*. Baltimore: Maryland Historical Society, 2004.

Silver, Peter. *Our Savage Neighbors: How Indian War Transformed Early America*. New York: Norton, 2008.

Soderlund, Jean R., ed. *William Penn and the Founding of Pennsylvania, 1680–1684: A Documentary History*. Philadelphia: University of Pennsylvania Press, 1983.

Slaughter, Thomas P. *Bloody Dawn: The Christiana Riot and Racial Violence in the Antebellum North*. New York: Oxford University Press, 1991.

Tanner, Helen Hornbeck, ed. *Atlas of Great Lakes Indian History*. Norman: University of Oklahoma Press, 1987.

Walsh, Lorena S. *Motives of Honor, Pleasure, and Profit: Plantation Management in the Colonial Chesapeake, 1607–1763*. Chapel Hill: University of North Carolina Press, 2010.

ARTICLES

Babcock, Todd M. "Stargazers, Ax-men and Milkmaids: The Men who Surveyed Mason and Dixon's Line." The Mason & Dixon Line Preservation Partnership. http://www.mdlpp.org/?page=library.

Carr, Lois Green, and Lorena S. Walsh. "The Planter's Wife: The Experience of White Women in Seventeenth-Century Maryland." *William and Mary Quarterly* 3rd series, 34, no. 4: 542–571.

Cope, Thomas D. "Some Contacts of Benjamin Franklin with Mason and Dixon and Their Work." *Proceedings of the American Philosophical Society* 95, no. 3: 232–238.

Douglass, Frederick. "Freedom's Battle at Christiana." *Frederick Douglass' Paper*, September 25, 1851.

Foster, James W. "George Calvert: His Yorkshire Boyhood." *Maryland Historical Magazine* 55, no. 4: 261–273.

Hayes, J. Carroll. "Penn vs. Lord Baltimore: A Brief for the Penns, In Re Mason and Dixon Line." *Pennsylvania History* 8, no. 4: 278–303.

Heindel, R. Heathcote. "An Early Episode in the Career of Mason and Dixon." *Pennsylvania History* 6, no. 1: 20–24.

Hopkins, Donald R. "Ramses V: Earliest Known Victim?" *World Health*, May 1980.

"John Randolph of Roanoke." *Connecticut Courant* 69, no. 3570 (June 24, 1833): 1.

Mason, C., and J. Dixon. "Observations Made at the Cape of Good Hope; by Mr. Charles Mason and Mr. Dixon; reduced to apparent Time by Mr. Mason." *Philosophical Transactions of the Royal Society, 1761* 52: 378–394.

Nash, Roderick W. "William Parker and the Christiana Riot." *The Journal of Negro History* 16, no. 1: 24–31.

Parker, William. "The Freedman's Story." *Atlantic Monthly* 17, no. 100 (February 1866): 152–167; 17, no. 101 (March 1866): 276–296.

Porter, William A., Andrew Porter, Ar. St. Clair, and H. Knox. "A Sketch of the Life of General Andrew Porter." *Pennsylvania Magazine of History and Biography* 4, no. 3: 261–301.

Powell, Walter A. "Fight of a Century Between the Penns and Calverts." *Maryland Historical Magazine* 29, no. 2: 83–101.

Sluiter, Engel. "New Light on the '20. and Odd Negroes' Arriving in Virginia, August 1619." *The William and Mary Quarterly* 3rd series, 54, no. 2: 395–398.

Torrence, Robert M. "The McClean Family and the Mason-Dixon Line." *Pennsylvania Genealogical Magazine* 20, no. 3. http://www.mdlpp.org/?page=library.

Wroth, Lawrence C. "The Story of Thomas Cresap, a Maryland Pioneer." *Maryland Historical Magazine* 9, no. 1: 1–37.

SUGGESTED WEBSITES FOR FURTHER RESEARCH

The Mason & Dixon Line Preservation Partnership website contains a wealth of information about the line's history and the locations of the boundary stones. http://www.mdlpp.org.

Paper Plate Education outlines an interesting activity to simulate the transit of Venus. http://analyzer.depaul.edu/paperplate/Transit%20of%20Venus/transit_frequency.htm.

World Atlas provide a tool for finding the latitude and longitude of your favorite locations. http://www.worldatlas.com/aatlas/latitude_and_longitude_finder.htm.

Photography Credits

p. 2: © Enoch Pratt Free Library

p. 7: © Enoch Pratt Free Library

p. 10: Courtesy of the Maryland Historical Society (MAP-1666)

p. 26: Courtesy of The Library Company of Philadelphia

p. 37: Courtesy of the Library of Congress

p. 38: Courtesy of the Library of Congress

p. 44: Courtesy of the Library of Congress

p. 61: Courtesy of the Science Photo Library

p. 62: Courtesy of Matt Wiesner/Northern Illinois University

p. 64: Courtesy of The Library Company of Philadelphia

p. 67: Courtesy of the Historical Society of Pennsylvania (Accounts—Charles Mason and Jeremiah Dixon, Chew Family Papers Collection 2050)

p. 72: Courtesy of National Museum of American History, Smithsonian Institution MAH-77301A

pp. 73, 76, 99, and 103: Journal of Charles Mason and Jeremiah Dixon, National Archives and Records Administration, http://research.archives.gov/description/5821514

p. 78: Courtesy of the Library of Congress

p. 84: Courtesy of the Science Museum/Science & Society Picture Library

p. 85: Courtesy of the New Hampshire Historical Society

p. 93: Courtesy of the Library of Congress

p. 94: Courtesy of National Museum of American History, Smithsonian Institution 74-1401

p. 94: Independence National Historical Park Collection, Philadelphia, PA, (INDE cat. #11891). Sally M. Walker, photographer.

p. 97: Courtesy of Jack Owens. Redrawn by Karen Minot.

p. 101: Courtesy of the Library of Congress

pp. 104–105: Courtesy of the Historical Society of Pennsylvania (Account Book of the Commissioners (1764–1766), Chew Family Papers Collection 2050)

p. 110: Courtesy of the Library of Congress

p. 111: Courtesy of the Library of Congress

p. 118: Courtesy of the Library of Congress

p. 121: Courtesy of the Maryland Historical Society (PP37-7-1-b)

p. 125: Courtesy of the Library of Congress

p. 127: Courtesy of the Library of Congress

p. 129: Courtesy of The Library Company of Philadelphia

p. 133: © The Royal Society

p. 139: Courtesy of the Historical Society of Pennsylvania (Correspondence—Charles Mason and Jeremiah Dixon to Benjamin Chew, Chew Family Papers Collection 2050)

pp. 142–143: Courtesy of the Historical Society of Pennsylvania (Account Book of the Commissioners (1767–1768), Chew Family Papers Collection 2050)

p. 147: Courtesy of the Library of Congress

p. 153: © The Royal Society

pp. 154–155: Courtesy of the Maryland Historical Society (MS174.1051)

p. 156: Courtesy of the Historical Society of Pennsylvania (Accounts—Charles Mason and Jeremiah Dixon (1763–1768), Chew Family Papers Collection 2050)

p. 164: Courtesy of the Historical Society of Pennsylvania (The "Christiana Riot" House, HSP Photograph collection V59)

p. 167: Courtesy of the Art Institute of Chicago

p. 169: Courtesy of Founders Library-Northern Illinois University

p. 170: Courtesy of Archives and Special Collections, Dickinson College, Carlisle, PA

p. 174: Courtesy of the Maryland Historical Society (PP37-3-8)

p. 175: Courtesy of the Maryland Historical Society (PP37-3-5)

p. 176: Courtesy of the Maryland Historical Society (PP37-10-6)

p. 178: Courtesy of Todd Babcock

All other photographs are courtesy of Sally M. Walker.

INDEX

Page numbers in italics indicate images or captions.